AF478442

RELEASE PROOF

Barmoor Castle map on page 206

Brigadier-General William Sitwell
"Deedle" to his children

Constance (Conty) Sitwell,
by Edward Wolfe

Bill R. Sitwell

Ann Sitwell

Conty & Ann Sitwell at home

Simon Sitwell

San Francisco, Paris, Southerness, Washington, Santa Fe

As Far as the Eye can See

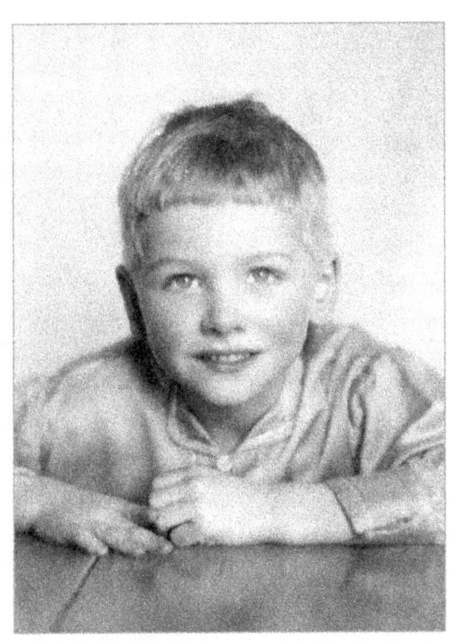

fire ™

First Edition: October 2018

A Non-Fiction Narrative
Front Cover: DFC, 1945

Design & Editorial
Elihu Blotnick

hardcover: 9781939434654
paperbound: 9781939434661

firefallmedia.com
literary@att.net

Library of Congress Cataloging-in-Publication Data

Names: Sitwell, Simon, 1920- author.
Title: As far as the eye can see : so near the mind will be / Simon Sitwell.
Description: First edition. | San Francisco : Firefall Editions, 2018.
Identifiers: LCCN 2018002553| ISBN 9781939434654 (hardcover) | ISBN
  9781939434661 (paperbound)
Subjects: LCSH: Sitwell, Simon, 1920---Family. | Sitwell family. |
  Northumberland (England)--Biography.
Classification: LCC CT787.S58 S58 2018 | DDC 920.009428/8--dc23
LC record available at https://lccn.loc.gov/2018002553

May 29th 1930) My darling Mama and Deedle. We had swimming today, it was great fun. I was thrown in. I can nearly swim already. I am top in my form, for nearly every thing. Please can you tell me Miss Leed's adress, as I want to write to her. I have bowled four people out in cricket. Matches begin today. There is due to be one today, only I think it is going to be scratched. Dash it all!!!!!! My pen has got crossnibbed. Anyhow there is not much more room. Goodbye for now. I am your ever loving Simon. X X X X X X

Two Decades

THE CASTLE OF TRANQUILITY *(1931)*

GENERAL SITWELL, retired, stood with his back to the dining-room fire eating his porridge from a small wooden bowl. Family prayers were over and his wife and children sat at the table enjoying breakfast while also chewing on the day's events.

It had snowed during the night, leaving the garden and fields beyond white in contrast to the dark, sullen grey of the sky; he remembered what old Charlie, the forester, had said only yesterday. "Aye, General, we'll be having sna' before the week's out."

The General had argued, as if he could command the weather, but the hounds were due to meet at the Castle that week; now, he thought gloomily, he'd better telephone Annette, the lady master of North Northumberland, to find out what she proposed instead.

Well, at least Conty, his wife, would be pleased and thankful not to be forced into conversation with the North Country ladies with whom she had so little in common. As an artful fox herself, she hated the meets.

The General glanced around the room. How invitingly warm with tradition it was: the carved table covered with white linen; the oak sideboard with spirit-lamps heating the white-clay plates; the finely prepared abundance of food. Nothing beat a full breakfast at the start of day, particularly in wintertime. His wife didn't agree but he'd had his way, by simply insisting that the children, still growing, needed plenty of nourishment.

The birds would need feeding too now that the bad weather had arrived. Their footprints marked the snow everywhere, and rabbits had been about. "Damned pests," he thought to himself. Last summer, he'd spent days making the garden rabbit proof, yet they'd been able to burrow under the wire netting. Next time he'd have to bury it as deep as a battle trench.

Conty pressed the bell to the right of the fireplace. Presently, there was a knock on the door, and the parlour maid appeared.

"Are you sure the post hasn't come yet, Frances?" Conty asked.

"No, Madam. It'll have been held up by the snow, likely."

"Oh, bother!" Conty answered, her voice shrill with irritation. "You'll bring it up the moment it arrives, won't you?"

"Yes, Madam" answered the dour maid as she left the room.

Thank goodness, thought Conty, that they'd be going South in ten days. She couldn't bear winters in the North, when it got dark at half-past three and none of her friends from London wanted to visit and stay. Watching her husband, Willie, she wondered again about their courtship twenty years before. He'd been a colonel then commanding the depot at Quetta. How handsome and dashing he'd been; such a fine horseman and as brave as a lion. All those medals he'd been awarded, though she only knew the names of two of them; one day she must ask him to tell her about the rest. Yes, one day; not yet.

She had to confess though, Army life after the first year had palled and she'd been glad to return to England at the beginning of the Great War. That dreadful War. Humphrey, her poor brother, through whom she'd met Willie, was killed, practically on the last day. It didn't do to think about it too much. Even poor Willie had been terribly wounded in the Gallipoli landings. It really was a miracle that they'd had another son, Simon.

And there Simon was stuffing down his breakfast, not behaving very well but oh, what a joy! He was the youngest and, she had to admit, her favourite. That golden hair, those pink-lit cheeks, and those pearl-glow teeth; how she adored him. She remembered then, barely two weeks were left of the holidays; she felt a pang. It was nearly time to take him round to Billings and Edmonds and see about his clothes for the new school term.

Ann, her daughter and eldest child, stared into space looking bored and wistful. Conty wished that she could understand her child, so as to have a better relationship. Ann was exceptional at everything; why Willie couldn't do enough for her; he doted on her, calling her "my piece" and telling all his friends how she'd got a scholarship to Oxford and had been called the prettiest under-graduate of the year by some writer in the "Isis".

Conty's eyes next fell on Bill who'd gone back to the sideboard for another helping of kedgeree. Her second child, he'd been born at the Army camp that Willie was sent to command in Cheshire when he came out of hospital. What an enigma Bill was and so different from her darling Simon. Bill often scowled in a frown and squint or sneered with a twisted lip and once she'd caught him being unkind to Ann's dog. But Willie thought the world of Bill; after all, he was his son and heir and would have the whole place one day. Conty was sure also that Bill was his father's favourite because he liked going out to shoot with the grown-ups.

She hoped that Simon would turn out to be more artistic like her, however hard Willie tried to make him love country pursuits. On Simon's last birthday, Willie had given him a small shotgun, they called it a four-ten, or something like that. Simon was pleased at the time but hardly ever took it out of its rack in the gun-room.

There was the terrifying incident with Dobbin, the Shetland pony, also. Willie had sat the boys, one at a time, with no saddle and only a bridle, on the back of the half-wild animal and then cracked one of his enormous whips, which otherwise lay about on the table in the outer hall, and the pony had bolted. It really was a wonder that either of the boys went near the wretched animal again. Yet only last summer, the children were persuaded by Willie to enter the equestrian event at the Wooler Agricultural Show.

They'd all gone, but only Ann was highly commended for her performance on Mumpty, a quieter pony. The rosette she won got pinned up in the harness room, to Willie's delight.

Conty couldn't understand this passion at all, for riding and shooting. Willie spent far more than they could afford on a shoot. About half a field, well, she imagined that the space would amount to half a field, had been filled with hen coops where John Mark, the gamekeeper, under instructions from Willie of course, put a lot of hens to sit on pheasant's eggs, presumably to hatch them out one day. Now, she looked at her husband, who'd finished his por-ridge and was busy turning the jars of home-made cherry brandy upside down, on a small sideboard in a corner of the room.

"What happened to all those young pheasants which you had in those runs up by the Moss Wood, Willie?" she asked.

Willie stared at her for a few moments before answering.

"They're wild now; no doubt they'll have found shelter in the coverts, where we've left Indian corn and barley rakings just for them. The birds will be alright, although I expect Master Reynard will have one or two for his supper."

That reminded him; he must telephone Annette now about the meet. What a shame it had to be put off; he'd been so looking forward to it and initiating Bill in the excitement of fox-hunting, and perhaps even Simon too.

"D'you mean to say, you let them all just fly away once they're big enough?" went on Conty.

"Yes, of course," replied Willie impatiently. It was rather a pity, he thought, that his wife wasn't a little more knowing about his sport. What an odd character she'd become. She loved beauty and shapely flowers, things like that, and found something to paint wherever she went; indeed, her art was outstanding; her water-colours especially. During a spectacular sunset she'd rush all over the house to find him to make sure that he saw it too. When they'd lived in Quetta, she'd gone riding with him every morning. She'd seemed thrilled with the idea of living at Barmoor when he retired and finding the wood spirits there, while he studied the landscape as a battlefield, for his book on border castles, including his own, but she was no longer always on his flank. He sighed, reflecting on how far afield she'd gone.

Her upbringing in a small village in Hertfordshire didn't help for starters. The Talbot family possessed very little money; not that it mattered too much, her father being the eighth Son of an Earl. The fact was they'd been brought up in a cottage-like atmosphere, where everything was rather shabby, until the father, an energetic and enterprising fellow, ventured off to Sumatra and made a small fortune. On returning to Hertfordshire, he bought a larger house and, free from the need to work any more, entered into politics to become the local Member of Parliament.

These days, Conty seemed to be well-nigh reverting to the care-free, untidy habits of her youth. Certainly her friends, whom she insisted on asking to stay, were a very uninspiring lot, singers and painters most of them. They were always exceedingly polite to him;

so they should be, and he rubbed along with them alright but what his friends made of them, heaven only knew. They were so much younger than he. None had been in the War, they wouldn't have got through their medical and probably were conscientious objectors anyway but hadn't the guts to admit it. No, he thought, a pretty undesirable bunch on the whole except for that young Australian artist. He couldn't remember his name, d'Arcy something or other. Not a bad chap, at least he didn't look half-starved like the others and his uncle had been with the Anzacs in the Suvla Bay landings. No use grumbling though; it was his own fault for marrying someone thirty years younger than himself. It was understandable that she'd want to have people of her own age around her and perhaps the dinner conversation of the local Northumbrians did appear rather banal after the intense Bloomsbury tea parties, which she frequented often in London.

Well, at least there were the three children. Nothing wrong with them, thank God, he thought as his eyes went round the room. He was seeing to it that they were being brought up properly with none of the current sloppy ideas. Yet, he had to admit that Ann might be very out-of-the-ordinary and likely wouldn't live anywhere in Northumberland when she was grown up. He hated to admit, really she was too clever. She'd shown him one of her poems. He'd found it difficult to understand, not a bit like Sir Henry Newbolt or Rudyard Kipling, but clearly sensitive and good.

If only Conty wasn't so bad tempered all the time. Well, cold weather and long dark nights probably had something to do with it, but all the same he wished she wouldn't go on so about his cough or the fact that he had to ask her to repeat herself so often. He was getting a bit hard of hearing; he'd noticed it himself, particularly when a lot of people all talked at once. Well, look at old Curly! What was left of him was more or less hung up in a bag in a ward at the Star and Garter at Richmond. The man couldn't see or talk or do anything for himself; it was a waste of time going to visit him any more, he didn't know you. He was lucky to have survived so long. What a scandal the invasion landings had been. Other men in the Lancashire Brigade had died in the hundreds, too large a number from dysentery and wounds not attended to in time.

Conty was saying something to him.

"Is it today that Bolam's coming?" she repeated, referring to Bill Bolam, the agent in Berwick who ran the Barmoor estate.

"Yes, he'll be here at ten. I expect he'll stay to lunch."

Mr Bolam came out to Barmoor infrequently when the Sitwells were at the Castle, as the General dropped into Bolan's office every Saturday to pass the time of day and talk about salmon poaching on the River Tweed or other topics dear to both their hearts. Today, however, he'd been summoned to go look at an old lime quarry that the General was determined to turn into a lake to attract duck.

Bolam had been agent for Barmoor since the War and often wondered why the family didn't spend all its time at the Castle now, but then he didn't know of Conty's fondness for London. In any case, being the agent for Barmoor involved little effort, these days. Only five farms were left. When the General's father was alive, there'd been twelve but the majority were lost to death duties.

All the same, it was a nice estate; well watered and fenced, with the farm rents paying for the upkeep of the Castle and gardens. The General had made a lot of improvements. Only a few years before, he had electric light installed and once he'd talked about putting in central heating.

'Mrs. Sitwell put him up to that,' thought Mr Bolam, struggling up Scremerston Bank in his old Austin Ten.

At the castle, the children were getting down from the table.

"I'm going up to Watchlaw this morning with Mr Bolam to look at the lake," announced Willie. "Any of you want to come with me?"

There was a silence.

"I don't think they should go out in this weather," said Conty. "I'm sure it'll snow again"

"Do 'em good to get some fresh air. We could take a gun and perhaps bag a pigeon. They'll be alright if they're well wrapped up."

"You won't go, will you, Simon?" Conty said. "Didn't you say that you wanted to show me the Royal Scot?"

She was referring to his new railway engine, given to him as a present. For weeks he'd pored over a Basett-Lowke catalogue for gauge O trains and then persuaded someone to take him up to High Holborn so he could gaze at them in the shop window.

Simon watched his parents not knowing what to say. He didn't want to disappoint his father but, on the other hand, he longed to try out the new railway track he'd assembled on the floor of the upper schoolroom.

"You stay with me, darling," said his mother. He could tell from the tone of her voice, that was the end of the matter.

"Alright," said their father. "Bill, you'll come with me, won't you? We'll take the car as far as the top of the West Drive and walk on from there"

Bill nodded. "Alright," he mumbled. He supposed he'd better go even though he wasn't very keen on the idea.

"Simon'll lend you his four-ten, I expect," said Willie.

"Why can't I take my own gun"? asked Bill.

"It's a bit on the heavy side for you if the ground's slippery."

"Oh, fine. What time are we going?"

"As soon as Mr Bolam gets here, in half an hour, I should think."

Frances, the parlour maid, appeared at the door to clear away the breakfast things.

"Will you tell Cook Hope that there'll be one extra for lunch?" said Conty.

The room emptied; the crackling of the blazing fire formed a background to the clatter of the breakfast dishes being removed.

SUMMER HOLIDAY arrived finally. Bill, like Simon, was in seventh heaven. Even Ann seemed happy. She'd enjoyed her first term at Oxford and got on well with her tutor at Somerville, her college.

What the children liked so much was that the whole of the holiday was to be spent at Barmoor. Holidays during the year were spoilt, by being spent entirely in London at the house in Grosvenor Road or at their grandmother's house at Hemel Hempstead. Even Christmas was dampened by having to go down to London before the term started. The exodus usually took place a week after the servants' New Year's party, when the whole of the kitchen part of the Castle was transformed into a dining-room festooned with paper-chains and balloons. The same day, after tea, preparations began. By the time the family went downstairs to wish everyone a Happy New Year, the party was in full swing. Conty regarded all of this as unnecessary, something to be endured and disposed of as quickly as possible. But Willie loved it and had drinks with the men and made a little speech thanking them for their hard work.

But now the summer holidays were here! Ann would not be around as much as she used to be; lots of admirers had invited her to stay, no doubt, but for Bill and Simon, the long days and all the lovely fruit to be pinched from the kitchen garden made life worthwhile. In the first week the boys overhauled their bicycles and argued over which wood to choose to build a new shack.

The estate held pre-historic oaks unplanted by man, but for the boys' summer ritual only small larch were felled and sawn up into suitable lengths to form the frame for a wooden house, which was then thatched with the bracken growing about in profusion. In the middle of August, after Simon's birthday, a sleeping out day, or rather night, was announced. Firewood and logs were piled up outside the shack, stones collected to put around the camp fire, and extra bracken on which to sleep placed inside the large room. Then, with excitement at fever pitch, the boys made their way, after an early schoolroom supper, to the wood where the shack waited.

With a bit of luck, cousins from Norfolk would be staying when the great adventure took place; and sometimes a friend of Ann's was able to join them. Bill and Simon approved of a girl or two coming along since they were good at cooking breakfast. Mind you, Ann had her uses too; she now had a little car, an old Clyno which she bought from Robinson's Garage in the village for seven pounds and had agreed to it being used to ferry pots and pans and things up to the shack. On beautiful mornings in the past, they'd actually driven down to the beach at Cheswick for an early swim. The sea was only six miles from Barmoor. Though the water was usually freezing, nobody really minded.

The past summer, the sleeping out treat had been awful though. Cooie, a cousin of their mother's asked herself to visit and insisted on joining Bill and Simon, who disliked her intensely; they could not stand the way she tagged along with them and always tried to be so funny. What's more, they knew their father could not stand her either. She'd never married and lived an impecunious life in her mother's house in Chelsea.

"I hate Cooie. I hope we'll not be lumbered all the time with her," Simon announced solemnly to his brother. "She looks like some mangy old turkey," he continued, warming to his pet hate.

"Oh, I dunno," said Bill. "She's not that bad and she gives me half-a-crown when she leaves."

"She must give up trying to draw me!" exploded Simon. Cooie regarded herself as quite an artist and liked everyone to know it.

"If Deedle had his way, she'd never even get down the drive, let alone into the house," went on Simon.

Deedle was the boys' name for their father.

"Well, she's not as bad as some of Mama's other friends," Bill pointed out. "All they seem to want to do is sit around or go out after tea looking for mushrooms. This morning I caught one of them helping himself to cigarettes out of Deedle's extra box in the green drawing-room."

"None of our friends ever get asked to stay," complained Simon.

They were sitting on top of the kitchen garden wall trying to see the whereabouts of Smith, the head gardener. Not until he was out of the way was it safe to raid the strawberry beds.

"D'you think he's gone for his lunch?" questioned Bill, "I can't see him anywhere." He'd only half listened to Simon on the subject of summer visitors.

"Dunno," answered Simon. The trouble with Bill was that he was just interested in getting under the net in the strawberry bed. "Ann is the only one who ever has her friends to stay," grumbled Simon. "Jolly unfair, I call it."

The conversation ended when they saw their father coming through the garden gate, a large basket under his arm.

"Bet he's on his way to thin the grapes," remarked Bill.

"Don't blame him," said his brother. "Dunno how he puts up with some of the people Mama invites here."

The very same thought was passing through General Sitwell's

mind as he walked towards the greenhouse. He nodded to the boys, but kept the thought quiet. He knew what they were up to.

CONTY SITWELL sat at her writing table in the green drawing-room, gazing out of the window framing the front balcony and the enormous lawn beyond, lush and carpeted round with daisies.

In the mornings, sun came pouring in, bringing all the colours to life. Glancing round her, she took in the beautiful Chinese wallpaper, the exquisite Louis XV furniture and the Bechstein grand piano, a wedding present from Aunt Margaret, one of the richer members of the Talbot family.

All four rooms in that part of the house were oval shaped; above the green room was her bedroom with its lovely view of the sea. Above that with a still better view was the upper school-room, which went unused for lessons, now the children were at school, but Simon had taken it over and railway lines, round which his model trains rushed at alarming speed, covered the entire floor.

Conty sighed, undecided what to do. Well, at least she'd got rid of her visitors albeit temporarily. After breakfast, she'd suggested they motor over to Bamburgh Castle to go for a walk along the beach where they could see the Farne Islands and the lighthouse from which Grace Darling, the lighthouse keeper's daughter, in 1838 had set out in her lifeboat to rescue a few drowning sailors.

How romantic and exciting it was here, Conty thought. So full of history and strikingly beautiful. Willie had told her that the sea had receded in the past 700 years, as ships once could sail around Bamburgh Castle; it was a sally port then with steps an only way in.

Conty's visitors had wanted her to go with them, but she made an excuse and ordered the car. Besides, it was rather unfair on poor Willie. He tried awfully hard but it was no use pretending that he had much in common with Teddy and Hubert, or Cooie; he'd never liked her either. I suppose he's jealous in a way, she reflected. Oh well, it can't be helped and he's happy enough clipping the hedges, while he's thinking about his new book on ruins and monuments, that he's in the midst of writing. What an odd man he is. So stiff and stern in many ways, yet absolutely worshipped by the children, with perhaps the exception of Bill. Yet, Willie never failed to read to them, when he went up to say goodnight, although the only one who went to bed early now, she supposed, was Simon.

She heard the clock in the saloon strike eleven. She really must pull herself together and stop dreaming. She was halfway through the draft of a new novel; she ought to finish the next chapter. So far it was better than she'd ever thought it could be. Her first novel, much to her surprise, had been acclaimed and her publisher, Jonathan Cape, had written to say that another friendly publisher in France now wanted to include it in the *Traveller's Library*, whatever that was, but whatever, apparently it was rather an achievement; she couldn't help feeling quite excited.

In fact Reggie, the lead character in *White Thorn*, the new novel, was very real. She intended writing to himthat day also. How strange that he should play such a large and true part in her life. Head-over-heels in love with him as a schoolgirl, she thought she'd completely forget about him once she grew up. She had, while he traveled abroad, but in the middle of the War they met again at Christmastime. She'd been shopping in the Army and Navy Store when she saw him in the book department. For a moment she did not recognise him, he'd changed that much. "Hullo, Golly," he'd said. "My Goodness, this is quite the turn-up!"

Conty didn't know how to answer; to be called by her nursery name after so many years, she felt herself blushing.

"Hullo, Reggie," she'd replied lamely. "I didn't know you were back in England."

"Of course, I'm back. You didn't think I'd stay away and miss the show, did you?"

"I suppose you're on leave?" she'd asked. A stupid remark, she realised, but she couldn't think of another.

"Rather! What about you? Is that a wedding ring I see on your aristocratic finger?" Reggie had always been an awful flirt and fond of paying compliments to anyone with a pretty face.

"Yes, I've been married for over four years."

"Well, I never! I didn't see it in *The Times*."

She wasn't to know, Reggie rarely saw *The Times*; only when he visited the Mombasa Club now and again did he ever glance at it. "Who's the lucky blighter?" he asked.

"His name's William Sitwell," she answered meekly. "He's in the Army; a General actually."

Reggie had looked at her in amazement before bursting into laughter. "What! I don't believe it ! My Goodness, you've changed."

"It's true," said Conty. "My husband's trying his hand at books now. He's just back from Gallipoli, he was rather badly wounded."

"Rotten luck!" Reggie pulled a face. He'd been lucky not to catch a packet himself.

"Tell you what," he exclaimed, "Why don't we go have a cup of tea at Gunters?"

Golly had nodded her head, and that's how it had all started, Conty recalled, sitting now in the green drawing-room at Barmoor. It hadn't been difficult to find herself in love with Reggie again. Boyish and light-hearted, always laughing and joking and telling funny stories, he was so completely different from Willie.

Apparently, as soon as War broke out, Reggie had come back to England to join the Army, but the newly formed Royal Flying Corps needed recruits. Reggie had volunteered, been transferred in, and taught to fly. Within weeks he was stationed in France and in action against German fighters. That's about all there was to it. On leave, he didn't talk much about the actual flying; he knew that Conty would be thoroughly bored. But he could see that she was very taken with him; probably it was the wings on his Army uniform. Most young ladies found them irresistible.

'Yes, that chance meeting changed my life,' thought Golly, just as she became Conty Sitwell again, still in her drawing-room. She'd better finish the chapter though before writing to him directly. But it was no good, her head stalled on empty, as it always did when she thought of him. Poor Reggie; so hopeless, without any money too. The Company he'd worked for in East Africa before the War was gone and despite his good record and Distinguished Flying Cross, he had no success at all in finding a job. Staying now in a very seedy flat in North London, he lived off his wits as best he could. 'Oh, if only I could help him more,' she thought, gazing out at the lawn and the man mowing it, who went up and down, the Atco droning away like a giant insect, even when paused, for the man to empty the grass box.

Indeed she'd introduced Reggie to Willie, hoping that Willie might know someone to employ Reggie. But nothing had come of it. Reggie was like so many other returning heroes, on the scrap-heap, to put it bluntly. Well, she'd see him soon and give him a bit of money and buy him groceries too. They might even manage to spend an hour together in his flat. Her heart beat faster at the thought of it.

The ringing telephone interrupted her anticipation. A maid answered. Presently, there was a knock on the half-open door. "It's someone wanting the General," said the girl.

"I'm afraid I've no idea where he is, Mary. Who wants him?"

"It 's a gentleman from Newcastle."

"Well, tell him that the General is not in and to try later," replied Conty in the special voice which she reserved for servants. What a bore it was being bothered like this, probably by one of Willie's lodge friends. She knew that her husband was quite important in the mysterious world of Free Masonry and their search for past Celtic spirits.

"Very well, Madam," said the maid and left the room.

Conty returned to her pen and writing paper. The novel must be postponed, she thought, and then penned the first words of her letter to Reggie. She couldn't wait to get back to London.

GENERAL SITWELL carefully placed the scissors he'd used to thin the grapes in the basket propped at the top of the greenhouse steps, before looking around him. A friend had said that the two finest vines in the North of England could be found at Barmoor. That didn't surprise him, considering all the time he spent tending them. He liked the black Muscats best, not just the taste but the full shape and feel of them.

He remembered long ago, when lost and nearly dying of thirst in Bechuanaland, all he could think of were enormous Barmoor grapes. His horse saved his life though, by taking him to water.

He'd been a young subaltern then, in the 1880s and had been seconded from his regiment to protect Cecil Rhodes, who at that time was building the Cape to Cairo railway, without proper maps, roads or even track. The army found its way about then just by using a compass.

Taking his hat off and wiping his forehead, the General sat down in the vinery and lit a cigarette. It eased his usual impatience.

When he was a young man, Queen Victoria had been on the throne and the British Empire about to reach its peak in prestige and power. The South African War had yet to be fought but no one had any doubt who the victor would be. Morale in the Queen's Forces was high and to be a young officer in a good line regiment was the ambition of every young upper-class gentleman then.

He had gone to Sandhurst after leaving Harrow and nearly been awarded the Sword of Honour. He'd been posted to the Fighting Fifth, as his regiment was known, and had spent some very happy years in Ireland at the Curragh before coming out to Africa.

What a long time ago it was. All his life he'd been on active service; he'd a good reputation and was popular with his men. They nicknamed him "Mad Jack" after his dare-devil skirmishes with the tribesmen on India's north-west frontier. He reached the rank of Colonel and was at Quetta, in India, when Conty came out to visit her younger brother, who was attached to the regiment Willie commanded. Tall and pretty, she made a hit with the unattached subalterns and yet, rather to Willie's surprise, it seemed she quite preferred him to anyone else.

Admittedly, as the senior officer with authority to arrange for her to have a good time, he saw to it that she had a horse and a servant to show her the ropes. Much older than she, he still cut a dashing figure, so different from any of her young admirers back in England. Her brother thought the world of him; well, he mused, what was so surprising in that; he'd a good family background and fine Army record, that not many could equal. Indeed he'd received his Distinguished Service Order rather young.

DSOs for gallantry on the field of action were also few and far between. Yes, he thought, she must've been swept off her feet. She smart show, coming up through the ranks." He found himself lapsing more and more into Air Force jargon; everything was categorised into "good shows," "wizard," and "poor do's."

"The only trouble I had," he added, "was leaving my battalion; fair enough, I suppose, as you can't be in the Sergeants' mess one week and the Officers' the next."

They fell silent for a short time. "Where's Cubby now?" asked Bill abruptly, addressing Ann and referring to her husband..

"We're separated. I believe he's somewhere in Wiltshire."

"Wonder if I'll come across him," said Simon, who thought the world of Cubby, in a hero worship way when he was younger; even now he admired him tremendously and couldn't grasp why Ann had ditched him. It seemed, she'd found his flying talk the last straw. Cubby was with a Beau fighter squadron then; now he was at Boscombe Down testing some sort of airborne radar for use in night fighting. That was the rumor, but the truth was he had to be exceptional to do that sort of work, and Cubby was superlative at everything he attempted. While he was up at Oxford, he'd been in the University Expedition to the Arctic, had sailed boats single-handed all over the world and, added to it all, had excelled at Science and Engineering. What a chap, mused Simon; a true high-above~average type.

"Are you getting a divorce?," asked Bill.

"Oh, I suppose we will one day."

"D'you like this school you're at?" enquired Simon.

"What?" Talking about her life with Cubby had distracted her. What a bore he'd been. Not a bit like the people she'd come across on her visits to Europe, while helping refugees. She could sit up forever talking to them; but Cubby's friends, all they knew about were aeroplanes and the War, not their weaker selves.

"Aren't you teaching at a girls' school at Bognor?" Simon asked.

"Yes, but I won't be there much longer; there's the chance of a job in London at the Ministry of Information."

"I wouldn't think you'd like being in London with the air raids," said Simon. "Where would you stay, with Grosvenor Road blitzed?"

"Oh, I'll find somewhere," replied his sister dreamily. Her own didn't hesitate, when he asked her to marry him.

He'd noticed her changing though, at the beginning of the War, after they'd returned to England. Travelling home on a crowded troop-ship wasn't much fun for her, but he put her discomfort down to finding herself a mother. She'd given birth to Ann in Ceylon on her uncle's estate. In England, he and Conty didn't see much of each other. She moved in with her mother in Hertfordshire, as almost at once he was posted to a camp, to prepare the Lancashire Brigade for the forthcoming 'show'. The War in France wasn't going as well as expected and the demand for more men was continuous. He'd his doubts about sending anyone over the Channel, but given his experience, it seemed more likely that he'd end up in Mesopotamia or elsewhere in the Middle East. He was right. When his battle orders came through, they were to embark for Cyprus and stand by. For him, it was to be Gallipoli.

He preferred not to think about those next six months; the heat and sickness; the mistakes by Staff at Headquarters. Put ashore in the dark with his men, he was more-or-less abandoned, deposited on the wrong beach, left for days without proper rations. he had to attack the enemy without covering fire or lines of communication. By the time he finally re-embarked, those left of his men were in a very poor way. He'd been badly wounded by the Turkish shelling too and had a serious dose of malaria.

He'd tried to tell Conty about all this; she'd listened and saw him in hospital but, and he hated to say it, she seemed rather unsympathetic. He wasn't to know, she'd quickly taken up with her Hertfordshire friends again, those she'd known as a young woman, but he knew that one chap, Reggie someone or other, paid her a lot of attention. He hadn't met him yet, but from all accounts he had a dubious reputation and his family was quite relieved when he took himself off to East Africa a year before the War.

Still, Reggie had survived it but disappeared, Willie didn't know where to, but Conty kept in touch with him clearly and insisted that Willie try to get one of his friends to give Reggie a job. Willie agreed to see him and even asked a fellow Mason to help. The chap had, after all, done quite well in the War and had been with a fighter squadron on the Western Front. So the General couldn't very well not lend a hand.

His thoughts turned to his Masonic lodge at Newcastle. Sometimes he wondered what he'd do without his friends there. They supported him through thick and thin and wouldn't hear a word against him. When it came to Gallipoli; those damned politicians, they'd never admit to anything; if things went wrong, it was always somebody else's fault. Half-a-dozen Generals like himself had got the blame and were given non-combatant jobs after the withdrawal, with no authority to help anyone again. Well then, not for nothing had the saying been coined: 'All's fair in War and love.'

Still, he'd tried to donate a stone monument to Lowick, but the town refused it as too roughly hewn for a war Memorial, though the rough and ready fighters under his command from 1914 to 1918 were much like that, so the General took back the whitstone blocks and erected them by the road near the Barmoor gate.

No use being bitter about anything, he reflected; he had three fine children; Barmoor was coming into it's own again. Still, how much easier life would be if they didn't have the London house! It cost such a lot to run. He felt the pinch, now that investments in South America had crashed. He'd been a fool to buy those shares, but money matters were a closed book to him. After all, that's why one had lawyers and people like that; they should've known what they were up to while investing his money. His father had told him never to trust anyone south of the Tropic of Cancer and east of Suez, and he hadn't been so wrong.

Suddenly the General winced with pain, worse this time. Again, starting in the bottom of his stomach and spreading backwards, it wasn't from one of his wounds, and that worried him. He'd better see a doctor and find out just what the matter was. He sat down on the steps and remained still, willing the pain to go away. After a while, he got up slowly, hurting less, remembering that he was off to Brittany after the holidays, to finish writing his book about early monuments, those places like Stonehenge and the Zimbabwe Ruins. Britons, who practiced Druidical rites and worshipped the sun, inhabited Northumberland originally. Ancient stone circles testified to this. At Carnac, quite similar stones were found and these prompted Willie to get in touch with Bernard Springett, an old friend, and suggest that they visit them. Although Willie was psychic himself, his friend had more extraordinary powers and was equally anxious to lay his hands on the stones at Carnac and spend a night at the site of the high altar. General Sitwell had already written to the Mayor of Carnac, a Freemason like himself, to tell him of their forthcoming visit. Willie planned to cross to St. Malo on a Channel packet and complete the rest of the journey by train. Yes, that was something to look ahead to.

Feeling better now, he made his way to the lower greenhouse to see how the melons were coming on. Smith, the head gardener, was there. "Morning, General. Seems to be fairing up some."

"Good morning, Smith," replied the General crisply.

"They say that Mistress Burney's away," ventured Smith.

General Sitwell knew this meant Mrs. Burney, a villager, had died. "Aye," went on Smith, "there was nowt they could do for her."

"Well, you'd better make up a nice wreath and take it with you to the churchyard," said the General. Little did he know then that in less than a year he'd be lying there himself.

SIMON, feet on handlebars, coasted from the kitchen garden to the stable yard. He'd had a good feed of plums and now had absolutely nothing to do, so he decided to see what was going on at the back of the Castle. He liked best to watch the electric-light engine at work, but it wasn't. Thomson, the chauffeur, was washing one of the cars, however.

Simon had asked his father why Thomson whistled under his breath while he worked and learned that Thomson had been in a horse-drawn artillery regiment during the War and that men who groomed horses always did that. He hadn't been in Gallipoli with General Sitwell but had served on the Western Front for four years. Once, in an expansive mood Thomson told Simon that his feet had often been wet for two weeks at a time and that he'd wake up at night and imagine himself covered in lice. Simon could only listen and stare, he didn't really understand such discomforts.

Now, leaning against the side of the garage. sitting on his bike, his feet idly turning the pedals backwards, Simon grew absorbed by the pleasant gentle whirring sound, the metal chain passing smoothly over the well-oiled cogs of his wheels.

"Will you be getting the sawmill going next?" Simon asked.

This was a special event, much more exciting than watching Thomson start the engine which ran the electric light plant.

"Ah divna ken that now, Master Simon. Mebbes next week."

Simon calculated that, with a bit of luck, he'd still be at home; it was awful how quickly the summer holidays were ending.

"Where's Robbie?" he said suddenly. Robbie was Thomson's eldest son who'd been born on the same day as himself.

"He's away tae Kailsay."

Simon interpreted from this that Robbie was with his grannie in Kelso, a town to be treated with distant respect located as it was on the Scottish side of the Tweed.

"Aye, he's away tae Kailsay," repeated Thomson mournfully.

He wiped the last of the water from the dripping Armstrong Siddeley on which he lavished such care.

Simon and Robbie were great friends and spent hours together bicycling round the garden. "Has he gone for long?"

"He'll be back the 'morn, mebbes," answered Thomson.

Good, thought Simon. There'd still be time to arrange a fir-cone battle then. Someone nearly always ended up being hit in the eye, but it was good fun nevertheless.

" It'll no be laing before you're back to school, Master Simon," said Thomson, almost reading Simon's thoughts.

"I'm afraid so," replied Simon ruefully. He didn't mind school once he was there; his grades were "very good, very fair, and very poor," he boasted; he disliked the actual return trip much more.

"I must away and get my dinner," announced Thomson, seeing his wife beckoning to him from the door of his house.

Simon nodded, put the bike into low gear and pedalled on.

The houses near the back of the Castle, where Thomson and Smith, the head gardener, lived, formed two sides of the stable yard. The building housing the actual stables was enormous, with twelve loose-boxes tiled in blue; a large hay-loft above; and an adjoining room containing glass-fronted cupboards quite full of harness and tack. The saddles and the rest needed, when pony-trap and chaise were used, were together in another space. The stables themselves were empty. General Sitwell no longer hunted, nor did Conty, ever. The ponies, used by the children, never came into the stables, being kept in a field near the Castle and even sheltering there too. A pony-trap was in one of the garages though.

In Regency times, when the Sitwells were wealthier and owned a lot more land, hunting took up most of the winter months. The Sitwell ancestors were horsemen of renown and, in the fashion of their time, great gamblers, wagering that their hounds could kill more fox than a neighbour's, or surpass a pack belonging to a landowner in another part of the country. Gold goblets and land alike were lost in an orgy of wagering. The Castle's dining-room fireplace was designed to revolve, exposing a second identical grate, ready laid so that the servants might quickly prepare the room for breakfast following an all-night bout of card playing.

General Sitwell was shocked by the style in which his grandfather had lived and by the amount of money gone, but what a marvellous shoot it must have offered. At one time, it was said, the family owned nearly all the land lying between the River Tweed and the Till, a smaller river that drained an area known as Glendale, but the estate now was a shadow of its former self thanks to the excesses of his ancestors. The General comforted himself in thinking that all that was in the past and couldn't possibly happen again. His good friend, Duggie Balfour, a lawyer in London, would make sure of it and Bolam, a stout fellow, such a help in getting the estate back into good shape, would keep an eye on things if he should die before Bill was old enough to take over.

Still, the inhabitants of the stable yard at Barmoor had yet to experience the luxury of a bathroom or an inside lavatory, and it was to be many more years before any changes were made, and a new monument to be erected, celebrating the weapons the English crafted and sharpened when they camped at Barmoor the night before advancing to win the battle at Flodden.

THE LAST DAYS of the summer holidays arrived. Not a moment too soon, thought Conty as she sorted through her clothes, deciding what to take to London. No such thoughts were in her husband's head; he hated the exodus from his beloved Barmoor. The only consolation was that he'd be able to get into the Royal Masonic Hospital on the outskirts of London and let them find the cause of his pain. The doctor in nearby Wooler wasn't able to diagnose it and suggested a visit to Edinburgh where the best doctors were to be found. But the General argued that he might as well be seen to in London as the family were going South anyway.

Young Bill meanwhile spent most of his day in a turret of the castle where, over the years, he'd established his laboratory, a dark and mysterious room kept firmly locked. No one seemed to know the history of this particular turret but, unlike the others, it was lined with cupboards and drawers in abundance, and Bill kept them full of beakers and retorts. Here he dissected frogs and mice, much to the disgust of his mother and sister.

Simon though knew that by the end of the day he was expected to dismantle and put away the "Barmoor Castle Light Railway," as he called it, which snaked all over the floor of the upstairs school-room. He'd delayed until the last possible moment and he still had to oil his bike. With a heavy heart he uncoupled the coaches of his crack express train and the mixed goods cars, pulled by his most powerful engine, sometimes even double-headed, and put them into the cupboard. He wondered what engine might pull the train south the next morning; it had to be one of the Gresley Pacifics, all named after Derby winners and all of which were quite successful on the East Coast route of the London & North Eastern Railway.

Through the open window came the sound of the stable yard bell, rung to call the guests in from the garden so as to change for dinner and secondarily to announce the imminence of a meal. Simon ignored the bell usually, arriving at the door of the dining-room just as Frances handed the food round. Today, though, he knew he'd better look slippy or he wouldn't be allowed to stay up late or have dinner with the grown-ups, as an end-of-holiday treat.

Ann had already left Barmoor to stay with relations in Norfolk before going back to Oxford. She didn't enjoy her relatives very much; they'd been brought up so differently. Ann was quite pretty, everyone said, but extremely shy also. She felt rather inadequate at big house parties and country functions that played so large a part in her cousins' lives. To her, all they ever talked about, it seemed, were point-to-points and race meetings. Ann was fond of her pony but she was no longer a child, and it wasn't big enough to take her weight now. Out of fairness to the animal, she'd stopped riding it. Then there was the after-dinner card playing. She'd no idea of the rules of 'Slippery Jane' or any game familiar to everyone else. While dressing for dinner, Ann wondered why she was so different, always. It wasn't much use winning a scholarship to Oxford but not having any of the social graces. Not for years to come would she realise that it had never occurred to her mother, to explain how to partake of the class-defined life led in other Sitwell circles.

Luncheon in the dining-room on that September day was a subdued affair, with only the partial family; no one had much to say. "What form will you be in next term, Bill?" asked his father.

"Lower Fifth, probably," he replied without enthusiasm.

"Well, that doesn't sound too bad considering the length of time you've been there," said the General, sensing that his son was depressed at the thought of going back to school. He, too, had been at Harrow in his day; then the school on the hill was in the middle of the countryside; now the fields ended at Wembley.

"Any chance of playing for your house?" he enquired.

"Might be," answered Bill. He wasn't bad at games and had been in the first eleven at prep school.

"Don't forget; put your name down for rifle shooting, will you?'

"Alright," said Bill.

"I'll be to see you, probably at half term."

The General's plans for that winter depended, though he hated to admit it, on that cursed pain in his belly. He hoped to goodness the hospital people would put him right. You could come to terms with bullet wounds, but this was something evil and more sinister; when he thought he was better and getting over it, suddenly, there it was, the pain so bad it brought tears to his eyes.

"Will we have lunch on the train tomorrow?" asked Simon.

"Oh, I expect so, darling," said his mother, smiling. All they could think about at that age was food, she reflected.

Simon usually managed to get his way when the last meal of the holidays took place. "Will you let me taste a glass of cider tonight, Deedle?" he asked.

"We'll see," said his mother. "Have you put away your railway?"

Simon didn't deign to reply to such an idiotic question. Of course he had. He nodded.

"Frances," she called, addressing the parlour maid. "Will you tell Thomson to bring the car round at ten tomorrow morning."

"Yes, Madam."

To be reminded of the departure in the morning was too much for the boys, who finished their meal hurriedly and, allowed to leave the table, did.

General Sitwell and his wife faced each other across the table.

"Think I'll go and say goodbye to Charlie," Willie said, almost apologetically.

"Alright, dear," replied Conty. She had to admit, Willie was quite marvellous the way he went to say goodbye to the estate servants, but he left the room slowly.

Conty sat alone with her thoughts.

1930

WORLD WAR TWO *(1941)*

THE STAMP of marching feet woke Conty suddenly. For a moment she thought she was back in Quetta with the soldiers drilling on the parade-ground near the married quarters. She opened her eyes; the mosquito net was missing, and the tin roof. Now, she remembered, she was in her bedroom at Barmoor with soldiers billeted in the Castle and on the grounds. She rose from bed and pulled back the curtains. The drive was over-run by men in khaki marching up and down, halting, about-turning and stamping their feet. Downstairs, a telephone rang; noisy voices were everywhere.

She sighed. Oh, how dreary life had become! This beastly War, how she detested it. Those horrid little men, who appeared one day soon after it started, had gone all over the Castle talking in hushed voices and scribbling in their notebooks. Then someone had been to see her, a rather superior official who explained that "they". meaning the Government, being in need of large houses, intended to requisition the place. Conty asked Mr Bolam to stop it, but he couldn't, and within days the Army appeared with trucks and guns and took over.

Admittedly, they'd been nice about it and left her a few rooms but used fifty in all for their headquarters and as billets for the officers. What hurt most was that they took over her beloved green room, for a sick bay, but they did promise to cover up the Chinese wallpaper with boarding so it wouldn't be damaged. Apart from her bedroom, bathroom and the children's rooms, all she had now was Willie's smoking-room, the dining-room, and the turret adjoining it, which was made into a small kitchen.

Conty went to her dressing-room to make herself ready for the day. All the servants had gone; only Thomson remained. Well, she thought, at least the house wasn't over-run with evacuees from Liverpool or some such place. The stories she'd heard about them were perfectly dreadful; most large houses had to suffer them. If darling Willie had lived, perhaps it would've been different. But he'd been dead ten years now, almost, and she couldn't remember the names of his friends who might be helpful.

She was absolutely on her own, with the children away at the War; it was impossible to get about given the petrol rationing, and London wasn't safe to live in with the air raids practically every night. Only a few months before, she'd learnt that the house in Grosvenor Road had been destroyed by bombing and the caretaker and his wife killed. Well, at least there was no danger of that at Barmoor; she was managing alright on the whole.

Cooking for herself in the tiny kitchen reminded her a little of when she'd been a girl in Harpenden; everything becoming more and more untidy and, she had to admit, more comfortable. Once or twice, she'd reached the conclusion that there was something to be said for not having servants all around. It was not at all necessary to clean or clean the way they did; they always interrupted her with their questions. No, on the whole she did not mind particularly being on her own. Thomson was so wonderful the way he came in every morning and did the fires.

What she missed most was having people to talk to. It was impossible to ask her friends to stay; the officers she came across in the house were friendly enough, but she couldn't really carry on a conversation with them.

She found herself thinking again of her darling Willie. How she missed him! She would have given absolutely anything to see his dear face again. How magnificent he'd been that last summer when he knew he was dying, so extraordinarily brave, putting up with the pain and refusing to take his pills, until he was completely doubled up in agony. She wished now that she'd been kinder to him and hadn't scolded him so much. And the way she'd deceived him over Reggie! How could she have behaved like that; she must have been mad. Well, at least Willie hadn't known about it, although she wasn't quite sure. When she remembered Willie's sharp blue eyes and how he had looked at her and held her hand those last few days, she wept with anguish.

There were no letters that morning. They never arrived when they were meant to, which was another thing she loathed about the War. She'd asked about this one day at the Post Office but they were very unhelpful, explaining that it had something to do with the blitz. The man behind the counter asked her if she knew that there was a War on. That really was too much. To have had her husband shot to pieces in the first one and now, less than twenty-five years later, to have both her sons in the thick.

She wondered how the boys got on and whether they were safe. Simon wrote very reliably, but not Bill. Of course, he couldn't write very often; having joined the Navy, he was at sea for weeks on end. She wasn't sure what he did except command a corvette and hunt submarines.

She worried more about Simon. He'd joined the Northumberland Fusiliers, Willie's old regiment, but got fed up with the Army and was now in the Air Force being trained as a pilot. She couldn't quite make it all out; he wore an Army uniform when he came on leave, yet she wrote to him at RAF Cranwell; apparently he was taking a course. He didn't tell her more because he thought she'd be too concerned. How odd that he should be emulating Reggie; the more she thought about it, the more extraordinary it seemed!

Well, if Simon did die, it might not be an end, but a beginning. Ever since Willie had died, she'd been fascinated by spiritualism. Each week, *Psychic News* appeared; a growing number of people like herself were now convinced of life after death. She couldn't have overcome Willie's demise if it weren't for this faith. With her sons in such danger she derived great comfort from this belief.

Ann was somewhere in the South teaching at a girls' school. She'd married just before leaving Oxford but had separated from her husband. Conty hadn't helped them much; it was a bother; she couldn't understand them. There they were with absolutely everything and yet Ann was bored and spent less and less time with Christopher, yet she seemed quite dotty about politics, no doubt it had to do with her time at Oxford. Instead of looking after her husband, who was a master at Eton, she dashed here and there making left-wing speeches or canvassing for the Socialists. When not doing that, she'd just vanish and be heard of next nursing Spanish insurgents in some hospital in Barcelona; or someone might say he'd seen her at the railway station in Vienna taking care of refugees from Hitler's pogrom.

Conty felt quite let down by Ann's actions. Ann was brilliant, no one questioned that, but so very unstable. Her husband, about to divorce her for unfaithfulness, was the son of Sir Harold Hartley, a successful businessman with an astonishing academic career too. As Chairman of an English railway company he'd asked Ann to christen ships; she and her husband had spent their honeymoon travelling round America and being shown a wonderful time by her father-in-law's friends, who ran the railways there. But then she rejected that; she ended it entirely. Ann didn't try to explain to her mother why she behaved as she had. She couldn't, unaware as she was of her mother's waywardness in herself.

SIMON PASSED through London on the very night a bomb from a JU 88A flattened the Sitwell's house. On a 48-hour leave from the RAF College at Cranwell, he'd spent the evening at Hatchetts in Piccadilly with a Harrovian friend, Bobby Taylor, who had kept in touch. Bobby's family lived in a very grand house near Kelso, and the Taylor boys all had gone to Harrow. Simon couldn't remember whether he came to know Bobby at school or at Henderside Park, the family home in Berwickshire. It didn't matter much; they got on so well together, Bobby deriving pleasure from teasing Simon.

The Taylors were far richer than the Sitwells. A Taylor ancestor had shown remarkable shrewdness by investing in mineral rights and the Taylors now received a huge income from the coal mines at Ashington, not far north of Newcastle. The Cytewelles in the 1300s made iron nails for the world at their foundry and became one of the great landowners of the north, but the farm rents they collected weren't equal to the mining royalties the Taylors received. As it turned out, the first Sitwell in the historical record was also named Simon, or so said Bobby seriously, for once.

Simon had joined his County regiment, but Bobby went into the Irish Guards. The young gentry opted for Guards regiments or else the Northumbrian Hussars. Few went into the Fighting Fifth, as the Northumberland Fusiliers were known, based on their fine record in the Great War. When General Sitwell joined that regiment in 1880, it was a different matter. All the young bloods in

Northumberland who fancied an Army career didn't hesitate, but fashions changed and the Fifth slipped in the smart person's image of a "good" regiment. Once people realised that other regiments had class, the local regiment came to depend to a large extent on officers posted to it from other parts of the country.

Bobby Taylor, with his background, was commissioned after training at an Officer Cadet Training Unit. In nice battle dress now, he listened to Simon's account of Air Force life, but his mind was elsewhere. "Why don't you come spend a weekend at Caterham?" Bobby asked. "There's a very fine pub near to the depot where you could stay."

"Yes, I will when I can wangle a bit more leave," replied Simon.

"I want to show you my new car," said Bobby.

Ever since he was old enough to read, Bobby had been mad about cars. He'd driven as a little boy, practicing in the long drive at Henderside. His mother encouraged him and gave him a three-wheeled contraption called a Morgan for his 15th birthday.

"It's a pity you can't buy my old one," Bobby went on, "I could let you have it quite cheaply."

"Depends on what you call cheap," said Simon, quite tempted. He'd been thinking of getting a car ever since a relative had left him £1,000 in her will.

"Well, if you're serious," replied his friend, scenting a possible sale. "I could find out what it's worth. It's up at Chipchase at the moment. No point garaging it in London and risk having it blown to bits." Chipchase Castle was the Taylor home in Northumberland now that the family had moved there from Henderside the year before the War started.

With Simon's old car broken down and not worth repairing, he imagined himself the pilot with a sports car and added petrol to run it. He'd heard it rumoured in the mess at Cranwell that all pilots in operational squadrons were allowed extra petrol coupons. "Yes," he said, "find out what it's worth, and if it's not too much I'm quite interested."

He'd always coveted Bobby's Talbot 10 Roadster and couldn't imagine why Bobby had gone and bought himself another; but then, Bobby was like that with his cars, always changing them.

"Any idea which battalion you'll be posted to?" Simon asked.

"I don't know. I hope it's to the 1st, with my friends," said Bobby.

They walked down Grosvenor Place towards the Officers' Club where Simon stayed when in London. The Grosvenor Road house was shut up except for a small part occupied by the caretaker and his family.

The sirens had sounded while the men were in Hatchetts.

Suddenly, guns in the parks opened up. A full-scale air raid was taking place. Shrapnel from anti-aircraft batteries fell into the street. A group of searchlights focused on one of the German bombers high in the sky. "We'd better get into this doorway," said Bobby, strapping on his tin hat.

"Quite agree," echoed Simon.

"Not very nice, is it?" Bobby said, addressing the man sitting under a small portico. He didn't reply.

"It's not very nice, is it?" Bobby repeated, raising his voice against the din of the guns. Still there was no answer.

Bobby bent down and, helped by the glow of the searchlights, peered into the man's face.

"Come here, Simon," Bobby said. His voice seemed odd.

"Christ!" exclaimed Simon, on taking a closer look.

"We'd better find an air-raid warden," said Bobby grimly.

The corpse fell onto its side, disturbed in its death posture by the vibrations of another nearby bomb.

BILL WALKED slowly away from the builders' office towards the wet dock. He'd been in Bristol for weeks now waiting, standing by his new command, a Castle-class frigate, built by Charles Hill & Co. and soon to be loaded with the latest weaponry for hunting U-boats. Meanwhile, she was overdue and nowhere near complete. It wasn't the builders' fault, or Bill's. The sub-contractors were late with the vital gadgetry; some of the guns hadn't been delivered either, as German air raids had severely damaged factory production; all involved were doing their best, working round the clock and, indeed, performing miracles.

Bill shrugged easily, glad that he had this spell ashore, while waiting for convoy escort duties in the Bay of Biscay: running out to Gibraltar, rendezvousing with a returning convoy, and bringing it back was comparable to life in an armed trawler, not much to look forward to. Just bloody uncomfortable and hardly any sleep for weeks on end.

At the top of the gangway, he ran into Jack, the chief engineer, a reservist like himself.

"Any news?" Jack asked.

"Same old story," grunted Bill. "Be another month, I should think." They looked at each other, each wondering vaguely what the other was thinking. "Just as well you sent for your old woman," remarked Bill.

"She likes it here, people are very kind," said Jack.

"Yes, they're a good crowd. We could do a lot worse."

"You're billeted up in Clifton, aren't you?"

"In a small hotel, not at all bad," answered Bill. "Stage people use it when they're here. We've had some good parties; Next week, Doris Hare and her lot are coming. That ought to be amusing."

There was a long silence. "You've taken all your leave now, have you?" asked Jack.

"I've still a few days left but I'm not bothering," replied Bill. "My brother and sister are coming here next weekend; it's a long time since we've been together."

"I didn't know you had a family," said Jack.

"I've a mother as well, but she's up North. My father's dead; died in 1932," Bill continued.

"Was he in the Navy?"

"No, regular Army. Ended up being a General."

"And you went into the Navy!" Jack sounded surprised.

"Well, my brother went into the Army," answered Bill. "Didn't like it much though; he's in the Air Force now."

"What was wrong with the Army, then?"

"You have to be 21 before they'll let you serve overseas; so whenever his battalion got a posting, he was sent back to the barracks at Newcastle; he got fed up and asked for the Air Force."

"Didn't know you could do that," remarked Jack.

"It seems they wanted Army officers to train as pilots."

"So he's coming here to see you, is he?"

"Yes, and my sister."

"That'll be nice for you. What's your sister doing; WAAF's?"

"No, nothing like that; she teaches at a school in the South of England. She's a blue-stocking type; get her onto history and you're finished. She'll talk to you all day about Anne Bolyn or some old trout; I find it very boring."

"Perhaps I'll get a chance to meet them," said Jack. "My wife's very keen on British history, she'd get along fine with your sister."

"Okay, I'll fix something up, but don't say I didn't warn you," replied Bill drily.

Ann and Simon arrived a few days later. "We've not been together like this since the summer holidays before the War," Ann said excitedly.

"Don't suppose we're any the worse for it, though" answered Bill sarcastically.

"I think it's marvelous us being together, don't you, Simon?"

"Yes, great fun."

"Will we be able to see over your ship, Bill?" asked Ann.

"Expect so. Anyone heard from Ma lately?" he replied, steering the conversation away from the lengthening construction delay.

"I'd a letter from her last week. She sounded alright," said Simon

"Can't be much fun for her being stuck up at Barmoor like that," Bill said reflectively.

"I think she misses London," said Ann.

"But she's quite enjoying writing her new book."

"Not much else to do, I suppose," said Simon. "She said she'd come to see me if I didn't get leave soon."

"I think you ought to tell her that you're flying," said Ann.

"I have," answered Simon wearily.

"What did she say?"

"She took it very well."

"Is it very dangerous?" asked Ann anxiously.

"Not particularly, not so far." No point in telling her about the fatal accidents; in any case, it was only the clots who bought it. For him, flying was straight forward, although he had to admit that his first night solo in a Miles Master had been terrifying. He'd forgotten to make sure the Kigas pump handle was screwed down tight, and the engine had nearly cut over the beacon South of Lincoln.

"What made you ask to go to the Air Force?" asked his brother.

They sat together on a park bench in the woods near the Clifton suspension bridge.

"I got bored in the Army," Simon replied. "What I really wanted was to get back to sea, but it wasn't allowed. I tried to get into the DBMS pool but they just wanted gunners; the only thing left to try was the Air Force."

"I think it was very brave of you," said Ann. "You'd never flown before, had you?

"No," replied Simon. "The first time I ever flew, they took me up and tried to make me sick."

"Make you sick?"

"Yes, they do that before teaching you, take you up and do loop-the-loops and upside-downs."

"And were you air-sick?" asked Ann.

"No, I wasn't actually," said Simon modestly.

"Did anyone in the regiment remember Deedle?" asked Bill.

"Only one or two of the older officers, and they never asked me about him or how he was."

"Perhaps they didn't have time for him," said Bill. "I believe he was a bit of a disciplinarian."

"Did they get their own back on you?" asked Ann.

"No, not really. The trouble was I'd been commissioned from the ranks; they'd all been to Sandhurst. Junior officers like myself had only gone to the OCTU."

"I don't see anything wrong in being commissioned from the ranks," said Bill.

"Neither do I."

"Perhaps some of them resented it?" queried Ann.

"Maybe," said Simon vaguely. "But I don't see why. None of our ex-Territorial Army officers went to Sandhurst. I think it quite a

future never worried her much. It was far too conventional to be concerned. A friend would put her up until she found something, that was all of it. But she had to admit, she could be over-vague sometimes. Only the week before, she had got out of the train to Bognor to post a letter at one of the stations and been left behind. Not that it mattered much; the trouble was, the guard on the train had found all her things in an empty compartment and thought she'd fallen out of the carriage. Every train to the South Coast had been stopped while they searched the track for her. 'Yes, it had been rather a silly thing,' she thought.

Simon looked at her. What a hopeless case! He couldn't understand how she managed at all! Losing things, forgetting where she was supposed to be, and leaving Cubby like that; she must be off her head. And her stupid Socialist theories. She ought to see some of the things he'd seen, while on tramp steamers, being fed on Board of Trade rations. Now that was the real thing: being a ship's fireman, living in the fo'c'sle and having fresh meat only once a week. He rubbed his left forearm to remind himself of the flag tattoo of which he was so proud. The men he'd come across had good cause to be Socialists. But they weren't at all interested in politics and didn't even know who their MP was. What concerned them was how much longer it'd be before they got paid off and were able to have a good run ashore.

Simon glanced at Bill. They exchanged looks, sharing the same opinion about their sister.

"You came down with a History First, didn't you?" asked Bill.

"Yes."

"More than I did."

"Funny the way you got all the brains in the family," said Simon.

"You're just as intelligent as I am," answered Ann, defensively. "It's just that you never had much of a chance, the War starting when it did. If you'd gone to Oxford like you were supposed to, you'd have done just as well as me."

"Not a hope, I've never read a word of Shakespeare and, what's more, I don't want to."

"Oh, come on! I'm sure you'd like him if you tried."

"No, I wouldn't. That sort of stuff bores me stiff, just like Church does."

"That's something quite different," said Ann reproachfully.

"Not really. It's all the same highbrow natter; bloody boring."

Simon had tried from time and again to improve his mind but he gave up quickly. What he really liked were mechanical things like steam engines and railways and ships.

"You'll change when you're older," Ann said.

"Hope not."

"What about finding a pub and having a beer?" Bill suggested, smiling. He'd had enough of this conversation.

They got up and walked slowly back the way they'd come.

BILL LAY on his bunk clothed except for his sea boots. He'd been on the bridge of the Flint Castle all night and his back ached with the fatigue of standing for hours bracing himself against the vicious roll of the corvette.

"Christ," he thought. "What little bitches they were in any sort of sea; too bloody narrow but then, he imagined, they had to be designed like this. Anyway, how much longer could this ruddy War go on? No end to it, seemingly; and the news getting worse; Singapore fallen to the Japs and Malta just about on her knees.

'Well,' he reflected, 'I'll be lucky to get through it, although I've a better chance, being in a corvette than a tanker or cargo boat.' At least he hadn't been sent up to Archangel yet: one hadn't a hope on that run if he found oneself in the drink. It was difficult enough keeping the ship from icing up and capsizing.

A whistle came through the voice-pipe above his bunk. "Yes, what is it?"

"Flares bearing South, about ten miles."

"Alright, Number One; I'll be up right away."

Pulling on his sea-boots with one hand while holding onto a grab-rail with the other, he wondered what it was this time, but it sounded like an aircraft illuminating the convoy, a bad omen. Arriving on the bridge, he announced: "Sound Action Stations!"

The corvette came alive with men running to their posts.

"What's the weather doing?" asked Bill.

"Wind freshening from the South-West; be blowing a gale by the forenoon."

"The sea's got up then since I turned in."

"The old man will want us round the back this time to keep an eye on the Texaco tanker," observed the Number One. "Isn't she the ship to make a run for Malta?"

"Yes," answered Bill. "Can't say I envy her!"

"Should be a signal through any minute now."

"Aye, likely," said Bill, reverting into Northumbrian, unaware.

Not until dawn broke, slowly and reluctantly, did the signal come through to stand down. Like so many incidents, this had been a false alarm; no enemy attack had developed. An escorting Sunderland aircraft had illuminated a mistaken target; a message informing the Commodore hadn't been received.

Back in his cabin, Bill lay down and tried to sleep, but it was impossible. He found himself thinking of his father, imagining what it'd been like during the many campaigns he'd fought in. It seemed unfair that he'd died after only ten years at Barmoor; long before he was able to see his lake being used by the flighting duck or the entries in the Barmoor game book lengthen as his pheasants multiplied.

'Ma put an end to all Deedle's hopes,' Bill thought. The lake was left as it was, half finished, and the pheasant coops taken away.

"We simply haven't the money to keep on the shoot," his mother told Mr Bolam. "Having to pay £70 indeed, for barley rakings for the pheasant's diet."

The tennis court had fallen into disuse too, as a new net was needed and the money for it not forthcoming. No doubt, what with death duties and without his father's income, his mother had just cause to be worried; and she made sure her children realised it. They might live in a Castle and have a London house, but little money was available all the same.

'Give her due,' thought Bill. 'She saw to it that we all went to good schools. What's more, I had a fine allowance while at Balliol. The trustees were pretty generous on the whole, heaven only knew how; probably due to some shrewd work on the part of Mr Free-land, the family lawyer in London.'

Simon hadn't done too badly either; he'd gone to Harrow and would've gone to Oxford as well, if not for the War. It was Ann who really suffered. She'd been twenty years old when Deedle died, just the age when she should've had decent clothes to wear and a little spending money. 'Yes,' Bill reflected, 'Ma had been hard on her.' She seemed to think it enough that Ann was very pretty and had won an Oxford scholarship. That Ann got engaged to Cubby and then married him surprised Bill, but he'd given her away, and it'd been quite a smart wedding at the London Temple. All the same, Ann suffered; he'd never forget the time they'd gone to lunch with the Lambton's at Kirknewton. Ann had an attack of nerves, with a floods of tears, as they turned into the drive. She'd implored him to turn the car round and take her home. No one could un-derstand why; such a fuss at the time. Poor Ann had seen another car arriving and the smart clothes everyone wore.

Bill was still thinking of the pre-war days at Barmoor when he fell asleep.

NUMBER 10 platform at Kings Cross Station, all London after dark was a place to be avoided at the best of times. Now, twenty minutes before the Night Aberdonian was due to leave, it was truly dread-ful. Men and women in uniform, laden with kit-bags, walked dis-consolately up and down looking for somewhere to sit. Simon on two weeks' leave was one of the throng but he felt elated at the thought of going home to Barmoor. Only the day before, a big-shot from the Air Ministry had stood at the passing-out parade at Cranwell, and in a brief ceremony pinned the RAF pilot's wings to Simon's uniform. There'd been a party in the mess that night and spirits were high. Some of his friends asked to be posted to the same squadrons; others, he knew, were unlikely to cross paths again. They'd be flying Spitfires and Typhoons. 'Never mind,' he thought, 'they'd all survived the course and got their wings; and that's something to be proud of.'

Like all serving officers in the War, he'd been given a first-class travel warrant. He walked up and down the length of the train, noting automatically that the engine was a Gresley "Green Arrow" class, with a 16-coach load, far too much for it; it'd been designed by one of Simon's idols, the engineer of the century, Sir Nigel Gresley, to pull fast freight trains, but then, the War changed everything. Now it was allocated to be the "Night Aberdonian", something Sir Nigel had never foreseen!

Simon went up to an official on the platform. He only wanted to lie flat. "D'you think there's any chance of a bunk?"

The official looked him up and down and gave him a wan smile. "Wish I could help you, sir. The bunks are all reserved."

"Who for?"

"Gentlemen from the Ministry."

"The Ministry, what Ministry?" asked Simon.

"It's the same every night, sir. The Ministries book every sleeper. There's nothing I can do about it. Orders come down from the top."

"And what about the poor buggers who're actually fighting the War?" exploded Simon, his cheeks colouring with anger.

"Wish I could help, sir. You could see one of the attendants, sometimes a vacant bunk doesn't always fill" The official turned away as some other passenger confronted him. Simon walked on down the train. There were six sleeping cars, but the rest were ordinary mixed passenger stock.

"Any chance of a bunk?" Simon asked an attendant he saw standing at the door of one of the coveted sleeping cars.

"I'd like to help you, sir, but they're all gone."

"Thanks," muttered Simon. He spent the night standing in the corridor until, completely exhausted, he sat down on the dirty floor. 'Why am I doing this?' he thought bitterly as he dozed off somewhere between Peterborough and Grantham. 'Why does the bowler hat brigade always seem to come off best?'

The long and uncomfortable night ended at Berwick station platform, when he saw the familiar figure of Thomson, who looked just the same but was wearing an ordinary cap instead of his blue chauffeur's hat.

"Thanks for meeting me, Thomson," said Simon. "I didn't think you'd be able to; where did you get the petrol from?"

Thomson gave him his usual mournful look before answering. "Ye mind the windmill engine, Master Simon?"

"Yes."

"They gied us some petrol for it each month."

"Yes?"

"Well, as have nae had to use much the now, what with the gales."

"I see, don't forget me if ever you have some to spare," said Simon quickly.

"Ah'll no' dee that."

"What regiment's at Barmoor at the moment?"

"Royal Engineers. They're no' a bad crowd and they help us sometimes."

"I hope no one's been into my workshop?" It had been hurriedly secured with a cheap Woolworth padlock at the start of hostilities.

"No, it's areet," replied Thomson. "Do you hear from Mr. Bill?" It's strange, thought Simon, the way Thomson still referred to his brother as Mister, while he, perhaps, would remain Master forever.

Thomson and Simon approached the East Lodge, still occupied by Mr. Henry, the lodge-keeper. Simon had regularly called on him to hear his latest jokes. Perhaps later, he would again.

"The drive's a mess, isn't it?" said Simon.

"Aye, it is that," replied Thomson, sadly.

"Good Lord!" said Simon as they rounded the last bend in the drive; the lawn with the Castle bisecting it was covered in tents.

"What on earth's going on, Thomson?" asked Simon.

"That's where they have their offices, Master Simon. There's no' the room for them all in the Castle. Fifty rooms no is enough."

Thomson stopped the car at the front door. Simon went into the outer hall. He saw with satisfaction that the riding sticks and hunting crops still lay in their familiar places.

Passing through into the inner hall at the foot of the stairs, he noticed how dirty everything was. The stone stairs, normally snow white in aspect, and flanked by delicate wrought-iron balustrades, still climbed upward, to form the sides of a quadrangle. Three floors up he reached the top landing, overlooked by a concentric dome. He'd never appreciated the beauty of this Adam interior before, but now, after spending two years in the drabness of Army billets and requisitioned hotels, he realised the gracefulness of the house, uncared for though it was.

His mother stood on the first floor landing, arms outstretched.

"Hullo, darling!" she cried. "Oh, you do look smart!"

"Well, can't say I feel particularly smart," Simon replied. "There weren't any seats. I stood most of the way here."

"Never mind, I've got a good breakfast for you and then you can go and have a bath and a little sleep." '

"It's lovely to be home; where's Mary?" Simon asked, referring to his dog.

"I let her out just now, she'll be back soon."

Simon spotted two khaki-clad figures on the upstairs landing. Seeing them in his own home increased his dislike and suspicion of pongoes, as he called them.

"There are soldiers all over the place, aren't there?"

"Yes, I'm afraid there are, darling," replied his mother, "but they're awfully nice to me and terribly helpful. I expect you'll meet some of them; most of the ones in the house are officers except for those in the green drawing-room. That's a hospital or sick-bay or something. I believe I wrote and told you."

Oh, Christ, he thought, this could turn out to be an awful leave unless he scrounged some petrol and got out in his car.

"Your room is just the same, though."

Thank God for that, he smiled

They passed through the enormous oval saloon, which now held the piano from the requisitioned drawing-room. The formal dining-room had been made a large sitting-room with sofas and armchairs placed round the fire and the dining things put aside. Leaves of the table were missing: it looked quite small, ordinary.

"Where's the rest of it?" Simon asked his mother, more for want of something to say.

"Thomson took three of the leaves out and put them away somewhere. I'll go and bring you breakfast, shall I?"

"Give me ten minutes. I can't wait to get out of his uniform."

"Alright, darling; call me when you're down, I'll be in the turret off the smoking-room; it's a kitchen now," his mother said almost apologetically.

"Yes," answered Simon. Clearly the only sanctuary from the Army was the garden and woods. Barmoor was most definitely a Royal Engineers regimental headquarters, and no longer a home.

Every evening, after the nine o'clock news on the wireless, Simon set off up the ruined West Drive with his dog to the Moss Wood, where the ferns were shoulder high, the peaty soil smelt rich and damp, and there was peace. At the woods end, the blue hills, the Cheviots, rose, standing out sharply against the greenish sky. Below them lay the shadow of Glendale, where the only reminder of War was the red flashing light of the aerial beacon to the south, and there the Kyloe Hills began.

Simon breathed deeply and sighed to himself. What a pity no one was with him to share the stillness of the evening. He thought about his cousin, Susan Elwes, who used to come from Norfolk to Barmoor before the War. She and Simon had great affection for each other once, but she was married now and had a child. 'It's sad,' he thought, as he sat on a fence watching the Cheviots grow darker with the approaching night, 'how the War has separated everyone. No one knows for sure now where anybody is anymore.' "Damn and blast Hitler," he muttered under his breath. Here he was, just 21 years old, taking part in a war nobody wanted. He should've been up at Oxford studying instead of sitting around all day waiting to fly and wondering whether he'd survive or not.

One day after tea, his mother abruptly asked him if he still thought a lot about his father.

"Yes, I do," he answered. "A great deal."

"He would have been very proud of you, darling."

"I don't think he'd have liked me leaving the Army."

"But you haven't left the Army, have you? You're still wearing your Army uniform."

"Not for much longer. I've been commissioned in the RAF, as a pilot officer. I'll see to a new uniform when I'm next in London."

It annoyed Simon slightly to have lost his Army rank and be at the bottom of the ladder again; in the Army he'd been a full lieutenant. Still, he reflected, he'd get more pay and once posted to an operational squadron, he'd be given extra petrol coupons. That in itself made up for the loss of seniority.

"Oh, I see now," said his mother.

"I went down to the village and had a look at Deedle's grave," Simon announced.

"Did you, darling? I'm so glad."

Indeed, standing in the bleak graveyard of Lowick church, Simon recalled that September morning nine years earlier. He'd been twelve years old then and been told to wait in the inner hall at the foot of the stairs while the estate servants carried the coffin from his father's room. He watched them manoeuver the macabre object across the landing and down the stairs. He could have touched it in the hall. Ann started crying. He himself trembled. Bill stood impassively, looking straight ahead. "For God's sake, stop snivelling and pull yourself together," said their Uncle Reggie, his mother's brother. A retired Naval officer with a terrible temper, he was feared and disliked. Instead of following his orders, Simon let out a howl and ran from the hall, beside himself with grief. Jean Gladstone, one of his cousins, found him and persuaded him to follow to the funeral.

The coffin lay on a flat four-wheeled farm cart outside the front door. At its head was one of Reavley's finest horses, groomed and shining. People placed flowers and wreaths around the long box with a Union Jack draped over it. When the procession moved off, with the children walking directly behind the cart, the flowers obscured the wagon floor.

Slowly, the wagon moved off down the East Drive, the steel-shod wheels crushing the sandy gravel. All the familiar landmarks stood witness; the East Lodge, the War Memorial at the entrance to the drive, and the cottages at the side of the village road. But they looked different. Nothing would be the same again now that his father had died. Later, standing at the side of the grave, Simon could no longer stop himself crying. Then a group of Freemasons appeared, almost from nowhere, sang a special hymn and threw branches of yew into the grave. As the priest scattered earth over the coffin, almost out of sight in its deep pit, Ann stepped forward to drop a sprig of rosemary below; she'd been clutching it during the entire mile-long walk behind the horse and cart. Simon turned to lean against the stone wall bordering the grave. Tears streamed down his face. His body shook with sorrow.

Simon's mother wasn't seen for several days; she remained in her bedroom too distressed to meet anyone except her children, and them only briefly...

"Did I tell you about going to see a medium?" His mother's voice interrupted his thoughts. "I go to a very good woman in London whenever I've the chance."

Simon knew his mother had actively taken up spiritualism but had never discussed it. "Yes," she went on. "I spoke to Deedle through this woman. It was really extraordinary."

Simon didn't say anything. What on earth would she say next!

"He's very pleased with you and with what you're doing," she continued. "He said that he and you talked together and had gone fishing down at the mill stream."

"What!" exclaimed Simon.

"He said that you'd sat together on the bank and fished."

She looked at Simon waiting for him to answer.

"I did have a dream," Simon began: "that we'd met to fish in the mill stream."

"Then you did meet him!" his mother said. "Your spirits met at least. He's not dead really, you know; it's just we can't see him all the time."

Simon knew, if he wasn't careful, she'd be talking about her new faith for the rest of the day.

"I do hope you believe, darling. I know you don't like Church, but I hope you don't think everything just ends at death."

Simon tried to sound reassuring. "I often feel that Deedle's near me, keeping an eye on me."

"Good. I'm sure he is, darling."

Simon would've liked to tell her about some of his close shaves while flying, when he wondered afterwards what had saved him. 'Better not,' he thought. 'She worries enough about Bill and me, without making her even more nervous.'

"Shall we go pick mushrooms?" his mother asked.

"Yes, let's. Mary would enjoy a walk."

"I'll meet you at the front door; I've got to see about supper."

Having heard her name, the dog rose and rushed to Simon. She loved to have her ears rubbed. She stood by his chair, looking up at him. 'What a beautiful animal you are,' thought Simon. She was a fully-grown Morrema Sheepdog, a rare breed with a thick white coat and a long tail. She resembled a golden retriever, but with pale brown tips to her pointed ears.

Simon wondered whether his mother would mind very much if he took his dog with him when he reached a squadron. He decided not to ask. The C.O. would have to give permission anyhow.

His mother was waiting by the front door, ahead of him.

"Where would you like to go, darling?" she asked.

"Oh, I dunno. Let's try the mushroom field first and then walk down to the quarry."

They started out, each with a basket over one arm.

"Do you remember the walks you and I went on when you were smaller? You always wanted to go to the quarry. Why were you so fond of it, darling?"

"I like the remains of the pumping engine and the old chimney. I'd try to imagine what the railway looked like when it ran."

"Oh, was there one?" she replied vaguely. This fascination her son had for old engines was so strange. He was not at all like her.

"I wish I knew more about it," Simon said. "It must have been a marvellous sight. Fancy having your own private railway running from the quarry all the way to the Berwick road! It was built by Deedle's grandfather, I suppose, before he lost so much money."

His mother couldn't remember ever talking to her husband about the old quarry.

"I'd love to know when it stopped working," went on Simon.

"I believe it was something to do with lime," said his mother rather indecisively.

"I knew that," replied Simon scornfully.

"Well, never mind, darling. I expect one day you'll find out all about it."

Little did they know how prophetic her remark was.

They walked over the fields, quietly looking for mushrooms. As usual, his mother was gathering sights and smells for a new book, but instead of tagging along with Willie now, while in her own thoughts, she had Simon to follow.

He in turn wondered about the landscape and how peaceful it seemed, when in fact all Northumberland had been a battlefield throughout history. Yet, a farmhouse nearby had been built almost entirely of stones from the Roman wall. And Simon now wondered if the Quarry or lands at Barmoor had contributed to it.

1927

POST WAR *(1951)*

Conty Sitwell put down her copy of *The Times* and went to the door of the drawing-room of her London house. From the floor below came the clatter of washing up. 'Good,' she thought; the charwoman had arrived after all; she'd been a little erratic of late; not that Conty minded washing up herself occasionally; she'd got used to it during that wretched War, but she did dislike it when servants didn't come if they were meant to.

She went to the tall French windows and looked down onto the small London square. What a stroke of luck it'd been finding this place, exactly where she wanted to be; near to Westminster Abbey and within walking distance of the Army and Navy Stores and her beloved Gorringes. The people in the square were so nice as well.

The house at Grosvenor Road had been rather lovely, the way it looked over the river; always something passing, like tugs and ships bringing coal to the Battersea power station. The Germans tried to bomb it the night they missed and hit her house, she'd learned.

What a lot had happened in the last ten years! It still seemed unbelievable that the family had come through the War without anyone hurt! There'd been that accident of Simon's, of course, but he didn't seem any the worse for it and had only been in hospital for two days.

The telephone rang; it was Ann asking her to lunch the next Sunday. "Thank goodness she's married again and settled down at last," said Conty aloud to herself, afterwards. At times she had despaired of Ann; always losing track and giving her money away to strangers because she felt sorry for them. Well, now she had a nice husband and a baby boy and a beautiful home near Regents Park.

'Let's hope she'll stay sensible for a change and happy,' Conty thought as she readied to go out.

Outside, she stood on the pavement, momentarily undecided which way to go. The charm of Victoria Square struck her more forcibly than usual. What a gem it was, and how clean and smart. Painting the house every two years was rather an expense at the Grosvenor estate, but the idea must be to do the same here, now!

Simon was sure to look in that evening on his way home from work, so she'd buy a bottle of sherry too; she mustn't forget to buy something for Bill's son either. In less than two week's time though, she'd be at Barmoor; yet that might be a nice change, she thought as she hurried along Victoria Street intent on her purchases.

ANNA MORTENSEN placed a rug on the lawn in front of Barmoor Castle and sat down to watch her son with Bill playing with the toy duck Bill's mother had brought from London. Anna was rather short for a Scandinavian woman but had a pleasant attractive face and curly fair hair. Bill had met her at a party in Copenhagen and after a brief affair, persuaded her to come and live with him here at Barmoor.

It didn't worry Bill particularly that toward the end of the War he'd already married someone else, from just over the Border who he'd known for a long time.

The Warings were neighbors, living at Coldstream, and friends of the family. While growing up, Bill saw a lot of Betty, the eldest daughter. Married, they had a child but Betty had a difficult time when the little girl was born. It died after only a day. Betty and Bill parted after three years. Each lived separately now, only ten miles apart. Bill had never brought up the subject of divorce to Betty; he found her a slightly frightening personality who, being older, invariably seemed to get her way and who, also being the stronger character, succeeded in driving her husband into a silent rage.

Now, while Conty remained indoors writing letters and Anna sat on the lawn with her baby, Bill went round to the sawmill to load a lorry with logs. Later that afternoon, he'd deliver them to people in the village who'd given him a £5 order.

He had to admit, it was a bit awkward being unable to have his son christened and remain surrounded by the neighbourhood gossip. Then again, nobody on the other side of the Tweed seemed aware of what had happened. He had no contact with Betty and never saw her friends, much to his relief, so he put the problem of her and divorce to the back of his mind.

His own family didn't appear upset either, except for Simon.

They'd never liked Betty, and Ann was very pleased when Bill told her that Anna was pregnant.

"Isn't it marvellous," Ann told Simon excitedly.

Simon said nothing, but he disapproved and went to Barmoor soon after Anna arrived from Denmark. "You do realise, don't you, Anna, that living at Barmoor with Bill isn't like living in a flat in Newcastle?"

"I don't understand," she answered.

"If you lived in any large town, nobody would be very interested in who you were or who you married or didn't," Simon continued.

Anna nodded and picked up her sewing. They sat together in the drawing-room, in use again with the Army gone six years now.

"It's quite a different place, this," he explained impatiently. Anna spoke perfect English and was not stupid, but she clearly didn't understand English conventions, particularly in an old-fashioned corner of North Northumberland. 'Christ! My father would turn in his grave if he knew what was going on; perhaps he does!' thought Simon, allowing for his mother's spiritualism.

"It's very lonely up here," Simon went on to Anna, "especially in winter-time when one can't go out so much."

"I know," the girl nodded.

"The people who live here are a pretty stuffy lot."

Simon didn't believe what he was saying but was determined to make his point.

"I haven't met any of them," said Anna.

'Nor are you likely to,' Simon thought, 'not at this rate!'

"I'm not surprised," he said. "Don't you think it might be better to live somewhere else until you're married?"

"I'll have to talk to Bill."

"You and I know what he'll say. Don't you see? It's different for him! He's spends most of his time outside down at the sawmill, that sort of thing. Then he's got a lot of old friends who probably regard the whole thing as none of their business. It's not the same for you. It doesn't help not being English either."

Anna and Simon eyed each other carefully. Anna wasn't sure whether she liked Bill's brother or not.

Bill had warned her: "He's a bit of a busybody."

"Bloody little prig'd be nearer to the truth," Bill often muttered to himself. "Why doesn't he mind his own ruddy business?"

Still, Simon did his best to paint an attractive alternative for Anna. "You'll be happier living in Edinburgh or Newcastle and coming here for weekends."

"What would Bill do?"

'Good question,' thought Simon. What Bill had done on leaving the Navy was little. Nothing of note, at least; nothing toward a fine future; a few small ship deliveries from here to there; a venture in the Channel Islands that had lost him most of his capital; nothing worthwhile. Simon had tried to discuss his brother's failings with his mother but got nowhere. She invariably changed the subject when Simon became critical. She also didn't mind learning that Anna was pregnant and proposed to continue being at Barmoor.

"I'm sure Bill could find a job," Simon answered Anna. "There's the Forestry Commission, and the shipping offices in Newcastle."

Anna looked down at her sewing. The last thing she wanted was to be left alone all day in this huge house while Bill was at an office.

"Have you talked to your brother?" she asked.

"No, not yet."

"It'd be very expensive keeping a flat as well as this house."

"But he'd have a proper job to cover the costs."

"And what would I do?"

'Here we go!' thought Simon. 'They're all the same when you get down to it; what would you do! You should've thought of that before!' No, he mustn't be too hard on her. She wasn't English after all, and it was his brother who'd got her into this mess.

"Our sister Ann invited you to stay with her in London," Simon said as cheerfully as possible. "There's a lot to see and you could spend time with my mother, when she's there."

Anna smiled briefly. "That'd be nice; I've never seen London."

'Most mothers would run away from having a son's mistress stay,' Simon reflected. 'But not Ma! She'd argue black was white rather than admit to anything wrong with Bill or his choices.'

"Well," Anna had added. "I'll speak to Bill and see what he says."

But nothing had changed. Simon's words of advice fell on deaf ears. Anna was installed at Barmoor indefinitely and there she remained. It was his mother who first approached Simon about a change, on one of his regular visits to her house in Victoria Square.

"Did I tell you that Bill rang me up a few days ago? He asked if I knew when you'd next be going up North."

"Hmm, dunno. I haven't got much holiday left, and in any case it's very expensive these days."

"Well, darling; he seemed rather anxious to see you."

"Wonder why?"

"I really don't know," said his mother.

"Why don't you telephone him at the weekend, when it's cheap."

The conversation ended then. "I must go, to catch the 6.18," announced Simon. It was the best train of the day to Horsham, where he lived now. Non-stop all the way, with a buffet car, not that he ever used it.

"Let me know what he wants to see you about," insisted his mother as they said goodbye.

SIMON hadn't found life easy at the end of 1945, when the Air Force demobilized him. He'd tried to get a job with Lloyds of London; ships still fascinated him and if he couldn't actually own one, the next best thing might be to work at a concern involved with them.

A few days after he was given his civilian suit at the Wembley discharge centre, he made his way to the insurance market known as Lloyds in the City.

One of his Harrovian friends, Alan Dick-Cleland was the son of an important underwriter. Like many pilots, he'd lost his life in a Tempest squadron while attacking an enemy target; Simon saw nothing wrong with asking to see Alan's father, having first written to him.

"Mr Dick-Cleland has been called away to a meeting, Sir," said the official in the hallway of the famous building. If you'll excuse me a moment, I'll go and telephone the underwriting box to tell them you're here. Won't be a moment, Sir."

Simon sat down on one of the benches to the side of the long passage which led to the market, to rehearse what he'd say.

A figure appeared and sat down with him. "Are you Mr Sitwell?"
"Yes".

"How d'you do?" The man then got right to the point. "Mr Dick-Cleland tells me you want to come to Lloyds. Is that right, young man? If I may ask you a personal question?" the man paused and looked at Simon. Simon nodded.

"Are you in possession of £10,000?"

Simon was taken aback by the directness of the question. He felt himself blushing slightly. "No, I'm not actually."

"Well, my advice to you, young man, is to go back out through that door, the way you came in."

The man stood up. Simon looked at him. 'What was all this about?' he wondered. "I'm sorry, Sir. I don't understand."

"Unless you've got the money to put up to become a 'name,' you'd best forget about us and do something else." He held out his hand. "Mr Dick-Cleland told me to say he was sorry he couldn't see you. He was called away to a meeting."

So that was that! Simon didn't question the advice he'd been given, this being his first encounter with a real City business man. Three weeks on, Simon shipped out to Capetown; a family friend had somehow found him a berth to South Africa.

"I'll be back soon as I've made the money," he told his mother as she saw him off at Liverpool. Now, six years later, he was back in England, undeterred. He returned to the City but was rejected again and after a difficult time was taken on as a clerk in another large insurance brokerage, but it was quite a struggle to establish himself; his colleagues, for the most part, were younger and more experienced, as well as more senior in the firm. Simon realised, the only way to catch up was to be more technically qualified; this meant sitting for exams to get some letters after his name. For three years he took correspondence courses, with most of his studying done in the train between Horsham and London Bridge station. He was perfectly content, as his wife and children compensated for the daily drag to London.

A few days after he'd seen his mother, he was working in the garden at home when his wife called from the back door: "You're wanted on the telephone, I think it's Bill."

'I wonder what's so important?' he thought as he walked across the lawn to the house. He didn't find out precisely, except that Bill was in extreme need of something special.

BILL AND SIMON walked up and down the East Drive at Barmoor. Three weeks had passed since Bill had asked his brother to visit. Simon had only reluctantly agreed. It annoyed him that his advice to Anna had gone unheeded. 'But when all was said and done,' he thought. 'Bill is the head of the family now, as he's inherited the place. He ought to act the part.' Simon was being old-fashioned and a bit hypocritical, he knew, but for him the old values and standards were still alive.

"Are you in touch with Betty? Yes, I suppose so. Then I wonder if you'd do me a favour?" Bill asked.

"Depends what it is."

"Well, when I cleared out from Lennel, Betty's house, I left all my things behind."

"What sort of things?"

"Most of my clothes for a start."

"Why do you suddenly want them now after all this time?"

"I've been offered a job in Newcastle and I've no decent suits."

"What sort of a job?" Simon could hardly believe his ears; had his advice finally sunk in; were Bill and Anna going to move out of Barmoor until they were married?

"The work's in a shipping office; you'd know them, Harrison and Shipley. They own a few coasters and do some chartering."

"That sounds rather interesting. Yes, I'll be glad to help."

"Could you say, you left some of your clothes at Lennel before going to South Africa?" asked Bill. "You'd stayed at Lennel a lot then, hadn't you?"

"Yes, I did." Indeed Betty's other brother-in-law had arranged Simon's passage to Capetown.

"Perhaps you can ring her up this evening to ask yourself over."

Simon wondered if there was a way to retrieve the situation, but quickly realised he'd have to keep his promise. "You'll need to lend me your car then," he said lamely.

A day later, he sat with Betty in the morning-room at Lennel.

"How's your brother?" she asked. "I haven't seen him for ages."

"He looks much the same to me," said Simon. Betty and he had always hit it off, but the situation was now a little embarrassing. In the past, they'd sit up all night talking about Bill. Simon wondered if he could've helped save their marriage; but he'd been in South Africa when they'd parted.

"I can't think why he went off the way he did," Betty went on. "He did tell me, he'd met this girl in Denmark; I wouldn't have minded at all if he'd only had a fling; but he just disappeared. All I got was a letter from Jersey or somewhere saying that he wasn't coming back. I think he's mad, actually. You're all a bit mad, your family, do you agree?" she asked, lighting a cigarette.

Simon shifted uneasily in his chair. How in hell to answer that! He knew what she meant, although to use the "mad" was perhaps a bit far. Unconventional certainly, but mad? He couldn't blame her for feeling that way. His mother hadn't even written to Betty when it happened, and his sister was positively hostile toward her.

"Perhaps you're right," he murmured eventually.

Betty warmed to her subject. "I can never understand why he wouldn't settle down here; it need not have been here. I'd have been perfectly happy to have lived at Barmoor, even if it's bloody uncomfortable."

Simon sat silently wondering when, if ever, he'd get the chance to bring up the subject of Bill's suits.

"I know Bill doesn't hunt, but he could've done something else," she went on. "I believe he was quite a good shot though and he had your father's beautiful guns."

Simon nodded. The mistake Betty made was to try to make her husband into a country gentleman. Bill just wasn't the type. 'Nor am I,' Simon thought, 'but I can manage somehow; I'm a safe shot too, and I do know how to ride.'

"I suppose I shouldn't have persuaded him to leave the Navy," Betty continued, almost to herself. "He was marvellous with his ship. I met someone, when I was in Iceland with Bill, who said what a good officer Bill was."

"I didn't know you'd been together in Iceland," said Simon.

"I can't remember exactly how it happened, but he was out of the Navy then and doing something there. I went with him," she added proudly. "But you know, he couldn't possibly stay in the Navy and be married to me."

"Why d'you say that?"

"Because of our ages. After all, he was only a lieutenant, and all my girl friends, who I'd been brought up with, married captains and admirals; it couldn't possibly have worked. Imagine what it would've been like for us in Hong Kong or elsewhere."

Simon nodded. She had a point.

"Is he still with that Danish girl?" she asked suddenly. "Does she get very bored? She can't have many friends? I feel rather sorry for her, actually."

"Well, she's got the baby, that keeps her pretty busy."

"The baby! What baby?"

Betty stared hard at him

"What baby?" she repeated.

Christ! thought Simon. Now I've put my foot in it. He couldn't believe that gossip on this hadn't crossed to the Scottish side of the Tweed. "They've got a son; it's at least a year old."

"Well, why on earth didn't he tell me?"

"I thought he had."

"This is the first I've heard of it." She lit another cigarette. Simon noticed, her hand was shaking.

"You'd have thought he'd have told me. For that matter, he could've asked someone else to tell me. Why the hell didn't he?"

"I suppose he couldn't bring himself to."

"But what about the baby? It can't have been christened."

"No, I don't think it has."

"He's quite crazy," said Betty emphatically. "I'll ring my lawyers in Edinburgh tomorrow."

"Why?" asked Simon. He thought he'd better say something, however banal. One had to hand it to her though! Most women would've had a hysterical fit over news like this; but here she was quite calm, though clearly shaken.

"To see about a divorce, you idiot. Tell him I'll divorce him the minute I'm able to; at least he'll be able to give the brat a name; or have they already? What do they call it?"

"I haven't heard it called anything," said Simon miserably.

He stared out of the window wishing he wasn't there. On the other side of the river, almost hidden by the trees, he could see sheep with their lambs, grazing in the field that swept down to the Tweed on the English side.

"Come along, dogs," announced Betty suddenly, getting out of her chair. "Duties."

The assorted collection of whippets, poodles and labradors, there must have been seven or eight of them, started barking.

"Go along; outies," repeated their mistress, opening the door into the garden. "You'd better stay and have some tea," she said to Simon. "I don't suppose you're in any great hurry to get back, are you? You always preferred being here."

"Yes."

"And how are you enjoying life in London?" she asked, settling down again.

"I don't live in London."

"But you work there, don't you?"

"I commute from Horsham."

"Oh, yes! I'd forgotten."

Betty went silent. "By the way," said Simon. The time had come to raise the question of his brother's damned suits. "Do you by chance remember my going to South Africa at the end of the War?"

"Yes; Eric arranged for you to travel on a Cayzer ship."

Simon nodded. "I believe that I left clothes here; have you come across them?"

"I haven't seen any," she answered. "But I could ask Nanny if she put them away somewhere."

"Thanks."

"I'll see about some tea," she said over her shoulder, leaving the room. After a few minutes she returned. "Nanny remembers putting some clothes away in Bill's dressing-room. You'd better go and see. It's the little room next to my bedroom."

Two hours later, Simon took his leave. In the boot of the car, he'd managed to put three of Bill's suits. "I've got them," he told his brother when he arrived back at Barmoor.

"Thanks!"

"She's going to see about a divorce."

Bill grunted and went on reading the paper.

That evening Simon caught the south-bound "Aberdonian."

'Gratitude was never one of Bill's virtues,' he thought before falling asleep.

"That's the third drink you've had and dinner's not for another hour." Bill glared at his new wife sitting in the chair opposite him.

Two years had passed since the divorce from Betty had been finalised. He'd been working in the Newcastle office of Harrison and Shipley, travelling there and back every day by train from Beal station, four miles from Barmoor. It was a tedious journey and Bill had to admit that the job wasn't up to much, but he failed to realise the company expected him to buy himself a partnership, or at least invest some capital in a newer ship for its profit to them; certainly Bill Sitwell with his Castle and farms should not have too much trouble in finding the price of another useful coaster. With his practical knowledge of ships, he'd been of great value to them and they, in turn, had trained him in the ways of provincial ship-broking. Indeed, it was time for him to talk with the company and plan his future with them.

Bill stared at the fire, his musings far from any Newcastle office. He wondered about Anna and how much longer he could put up with her! Only a few months before, he'd left her at Barmoor and spent a week at Brighton with Campbell Mitchell-Cotts and his associates: "I'll be down to the beach with my circle of friends. Why not join us? The change'll do you good," Campbell insisted.

It was a wild and amusing visit. Campbell knew lots of actors and actresses, having played small parts himself over the years, but he didn't take an acting career seriously; he was rich enough to only work when he felt like it. He was a marvellous host, a lovable character too, and his London parties were inevitably spectacular.

The Sitwell family had always fascinated him. He'd admired the old General; a patriot through and through. Campbell had talked to him for hours about his adventures in the Khyber Pass, the Ashanti campaign, and the relief of Mafeking. Never mind the rights and wrongs of the battles; General Sitwell, in retirement, still knew his wars; he'd been there and his chestful of campaign medals proved he'd been a hero of the Empire.

Conty too had intrigued Campbell ever since he'd met her; his mother had been a friend of hers. "Everyone knows," he'd say to all, "that Conty Sitwell is a fish out of water at Barmoor."

Conty's novels expressed the lush mysticism of India in painterly phrases and made it quite obvious, she had little in common with the tweedy, horsey women of the North, who were rarely parted from their Cairn Terriers and Jack Russells.

Far from home, at Robin Monckton's beautiful, large Brighton flat, Campbell introduced Bill to a crowd of famous actresses.

"I want you to meet a very best friend of mine. You've all heard of the Sitwells, haven't you?" Campbell said, looking round at the people he'd cornered. His gold-mounted monocle glinting in the subdued lights of Robin's flat, he grasped Bill's arm and faced him. Like most actors, Campbell was never really off-stage.

"Of course we have, darling," two of the audience chorused.

"Well, my dears, this is one of them. This is Bill. He has the most beautiful house in the North of England. Haven't you, Bill?

Bill didn't know what to say. He'd been out of things for so long that he couldn't think of an amusing answer or slick response. He pulled a face, shrugged his shoulders, and said, "You'd better come to see for yourselves."

"What a marvellous idea!" said Campbell. Then, dropping his voice, he added in a stage whisper, "But not while you've got that dreadful woman there."

Bill felt himself colouring. He'd got rather carried away by a roly-poly-shaping luncheon with Campbell the day before and had confessed to him how bored he'd become with Anna's inertia.

One of the women drew Bill aside.

"Tell me more about this beautiful house of yours."

"It's an old Border keep that's been added to over the years. My family have been there a long time. It's half-way between Newcastle and Edinburgh, about sixty miles south, just inside England."

"Edinburgh? I shall be playing at Edinburgh next summer; may I come and stay?"

Bill looked her up and down. She was attractive, if perhaps a little-too made-up; but then all actresses were prone to be.

"Of course; I'll tell Campbell to bring you on your way up."

And so started the romance between Bill and Penelope.

He returned to Barmoor and carried on with his job in Newcastle, realising that it was only a matter of time before he parted company with Harrison and Shipley. He'd guessed, that they were waiting for an approach from him but it was out of the question; he had no money.

It was also obvious to him that he couldn't go on living with Anna; perhaps Ann could talk to her and suggest that she'd be happier far away from him; she'd started drinking on realising all too clearly that her husband had no further use for her. He was completely uninterested in anything that she or the little boy said or did. He didn't really talk to her anymore, nor take her anywhere; it was even an open effort for him to be polite to her.

"I'd like to go to London for a few days; would you mind?" she asked. 'She must be a mind-reader,' thought Bill. "I could stay with Ann. She always said I could go there if ever I was in the city."

"Good idea," said Bill. 'I'll ring her up and tell her.'

A week passed. Anna went to London, taking the boy with her.

Soon afterward, Ann telephoned.

"I've talked to Anna," she announced. "I must say, Bill, you don't seem to have been behaving very well."

Bill said nothing.

" I think it'd be better if you separated for a bit," she went on. "Anna wants to get away from Barmoor and I must say I rather agree with her. If I found her a flat, would you pay for it and give her some income?"

"I suppose so," Bill answered. God knows how; but anything rather than have the damned woman at Barmoor with him.

"Well, if that's alright, I'll send for her things and see if I can't find somewhere for her to live. She's pretty miserable, you know."

"I daresay she is," replied Bill flatly.

ANNA HAD been gone a year, and Bill left Harrison and Shipley to stay at Barmoor all the time now. By selling two paintings, he'd managed, albeit only on a temporary basis, to provide for Anna, his next soon-to-be ex-wife and son, but at least he didn't have to worry for the time being. He'd heard that the National Coal Board was looking for supplies of pit prop lids, as they were known, and he'd managed to get a contract to supply a few loads every week.

He wondered why he'd never thought of it before! The Barmoor estate had masses of timber, a lot of it softwood that could be sold to the Coal Board in various forms. Bill installed a larger sawmill and took on extra men. His money problems seemed at an end.

That summer, Campbell Cotts came to stay, together with three of his friends, and Penelope. The weather remained fine during their visit and Bill enjoyed being the host. Penelope didn't take long to move into his room and help him entertain.

No one took notice, that Bill never asked his neighbours over to meals or parties. Whenever the subject was raised, he'd make an excuse; he felt there was hardly anyone locally he could ask to his house! He fitted into the social scene less than his mother before him, but for different reasons. Conty Sitwell found the people boring. Bill found them intimidating and superior. They made him nervous with their tales of wonderful shoots and the hunting field. It was common knowledge, to add to that, that he'd lived with a foreign girl in his house and fathered her child. That finished him off with the County. To behave like that was beyond the pale, whatever the rights and wrongs!

Bill amused his guests by taking them for expeditions to the Farne Islands and other lovely places, but he was careful not to cross the Border; the thought of being confronted by Betty or any of her friends made his flesh creep.

So far as Campbell and Penelope were concerned, Bill could do no wrong. They found him attractive and entertaining, a wonderful story-teller and more original than anyone they'd ever come across, or so they told him.

"Tell us about that witch-doctor you saw in Freetown, darling."

"How did you get that terrible scar on your arm, darling?"

"Weren't you nearly drowned rescuing a drunken sailor?"

Bill revelled in it. He'd hold forth to his audience after dinner over glass after glass of port and brandy. No one appeared for breakfast the next morning, until long after all was cleared away.

When the time came for his guests to leave and travel on to Edinburgh, Bill was dismayed to find himself alone.

"Promise you'll all come and stay again on your way south," he insisted.

"I'm afraid we shan't be able to," Campbell replied.

"I expect I could," said Penelope, squeezing Bill's hand.

Campbell smiled. "You don't deserve her, you old rogue."

Bill laughed.

"She can stay here as long as she likes, as far as I'm concerned."

"Don't listen to Campbell here, darling; he's jealous, that's all! Aren't you, darling?"

Bill brought the conversation to a close. "You'd better get going or you'll miss the train. Thomson will drive you to the Berwick station. I'm afraid I have to stay here; there's someone from the Coal Board coming to see me about all my Collingwood trees."

He watched the car disappear down the East Drive. The house seemed very empty without them; what a noisy lot they'd been. Still, it'd been bloody good fun, worth every minute. God knows how much they'd drunk!

Bill walked up the stairs, a heavy blanket of depression making itself felt. 'One day she'll find out the truth,' he thought in despair. 'Because I live in a Castle and own some land, they think I'm rich. Little do they know!'

Some of the beautiful things in the saloon now had to be sold; with the party over, he was broke. Only the day before he'd had a letter from his bank manager about an overdraft, and he was due to give Anna more money. Then there were the school fees in Eastbourne for the boy. Oh, Christ! He buried his face in his hands then gloomily poured himself a drink.

Later that summer, Penelope came to stay again; this time by herself. By now, Bill was quite infatuated with her. This West End star who had played on Broadway and whose name had been on everyone's slips, loved him; or so she said. He couldn't believe it but it seemed to be true. "She's absolutely dazzled by you, old boy," Campbell had said.

When it came to facing up to unpleasant facts, Bill took after his mother; he simply couldn't help himself. Don't do anything today that can be put off till tomorrow, was the easiest of guides. But the evening after Penelope arrived, he found himself in deep water. "How many farms are there on the estate?" she asked.

"Let's see," he murmured. "There's Brackenside, Barmoor Mill, Moss Hall, about five...four thousand acres in all."

"I suppose they're worth quite a bit," she said.

"Yes, quite a bit." But they'd be worth a hell of a lot more if he'd only listened to his bloody little brother, he thought. That little sod had come up a few years before, to tell him he ought to end all his tenancies before the new Landlord and Tenant Act came into force. "If you don't give them notice now and renegotiate the leases, you'll be stuck with the same ones forever," Simon had said.

"What are you talking about?"

"I know for a fact, a new law's coming in; hasn't Mr Bolam said anything about it?"

"Maybe he has," answered Bill sullenly. This young brother of his was just a bloody little know-all. Why didn't he mind his own damned business instead of spouting this stuff at him? Bill nearly told him so.

"You'll not be able to get your farms back or alter the rents in any significant way if you don't do something quickly," Simon said.

"Alright, alright. I'll ask Bolam about it," Bill had replied wearily.

However, he had done nothing, and Simon's prophecy came true. The rents were virtually frozen and the tenancy went automatically to the tenant's son under the new law; the value of the land was halved, at the least. Still, they were worth quite a bit. "Yes," he repeated. "I suppose I can boast about them!" All too quickly he regretted doing so.

"Campbell always said you were quite rich, darling."

Penelope pulled her skirt up a little and crossed her legs. She knew how much Bill admired them. "I hate asking you to help, darling; but I'm terribly broke," she said.

Bill stared at her.

Normally, he'd have said, "Tough luck!" or something equally appropriate. But that wouldn't do in this situation.

"How broke?" he asked.

"About thirty thousand."

"What?"

"I owe the bank thirty thousand pounds," said Penelope coolly.

Bill was staggered. Good God, he thought wildly. How could anyone get themselves into debt like that! "That's rather a lot, isn't it?" he answered.

"I know, darling, it is. Peter always said he'd pay my bills, but he lost all his money when British Leyland collapsed."

Bill shrewdly realised that she meant Bill to be the sucker who picked up the pieces for her husband.

"I'll see what I can do," he heard himself saying. Even as he said it, he knew that what he was promising the impossible, but he was unable to tell her the truth; he absolutely could not tell her: he had nothing; thirty thousand pounds was a bloody fortune.

And yet...he glanced out of the window. All this land...this place...not to mention everything in it. And all that lead on the roof... he'd been told it was worth a thousand pounds a ton...Yes, he was a damned sight better off than he realised. He totted up his assets in his head. "How serious is it?" he asked.

"The Bank wants to see me when I'm next in London. They're being very difficult." Bill sighed, as he'd experienced the same thing but not on such a grand scale.

"You do love me, don't you, darling?" She rose from her chair and went to him. "It's only a temporary thing. I've got this part in a new revue of Desmond's. I'm sure I'll be able to pay you back."

"O.K. I'll see if I can get it squared off," he said.

"Oh, darling! You are marvelous! I knew you'd help me. Tell you what; let's open a bottle of champagne to celebrate."

What the hell, Bill wondered, later that night as he lay in her arms, exhausted by the events of the day. I've got plenty of money; the bank will be only too pleased to help me out. In any case, she said she'd pay me back.

'She said she would pay me back,' he repeated to himself the following morning; the phrase reassured him.

"About that money," she said at breakfast. "You will let me know soonish, won't you darling?"

"I'll go and see the bank next time I'm in Berwick."

"Couldn't you ring them up now?"

"I'd rather go and talk to them."

"Shall I come with you?"

"I'd rather see Mr Roberts on my own," he replied.

Before Penelope left, the bank loan was arranged, much more easily than he'd imagined. He had to hand over the deed to one of the farms as security, but Mr Bolam saw to that. It puzzled Bill. The bank manager was continually reminding him about his overdraft, but here they were, quite happy to advance him £30,000 against the security of just one of the farms. He really was richer than he thought!

Penelope couldn't believe her good fortune.

"Oh, you are an absolute darling," she said as she departed for London. "You are quite the most darlingest man I've ever met."

Bill stood on Berwick station platform watching the train pull out, knowing he'd made a terrible mistake, all that money, he'd never see it again, but it made him feel as if he really was someone. Yes, he was Bill Sitwell of Barmoor Castle when all was said and done.

"Bill will help you out," he imagined her friends saying.

"He's one of those quieter chaps but worth a hell of a lot. D'you know, old boy; he gave Penelope £30,000 just like that! He must be absolutely loaded. She'd tried all her rich boyfriends first but they weren't having any; yet Bill was able to help her on her way."

Alone once more, he busied himself with the sawmill and the National Coal Board's custom. Then quite unexpectedly, a letter arrived from Roger Bancroft whom Bill had known at Oxford: "I shall be passing quite close to you next week on my way to Perth and wonder if I could break my journey for a day or two?"

Roger had read Science and was now a geologist with a South African company. He'd kept in touch with Bill all through the War, but it'd been difficult to meet as Roger lived in Johannesburg.

If he's on leave, thought Bill, a little company would be nice; they could talk about the old days, without despair.

On the first day of Roger's visit, they walked about the estate.

"They used to mine coal here, you know," Bill said. "I've got a map somewhere with the old mine shafts marked on it."

"I'd like to see that."

"I'll have a look for it when we get back."

"Why were they closed down?"

"Flooding mainly. It was pretty poor quality stuff anyway; made a lot of ash but not much heat. The old forester on the estate, he's dead now, used to work at one of them. He was the fireman. One day he arrived late. The pumps had stopped. And that was that!"

"Good Lord!" exclaimed Roger.

"You can see where the mine was." Bill pointed in the direction of the south moor. "There's a wall round the shaft opening, put up to stop sheep falling down it. Some of the mines had their shafts covered up with railway sleepers with just earth on top. They are absolute death traps now because the sleepers have rotted away."

"And your family owned them all?" asked Roger.

"Yes, there were at least a dozen. Biteabout was the last one to close, in 1916, I think."

"I'd love to go down one of them."

"They're all flooded."

"What a pity."

"But I can show you the lime workings; they'll interest you."

"Lime? Really?"

"Yes, a lot of that went on as well. Old lime-kilns are all about."

"I suppose they dug the lime out?"

"Yes, they quarried it. If you like, I'll take you down one later."

"Why d'you think they stopped?"

"I suppose they couldn't sell the stuff. They stopped years ago. It must have been quite an operation; there was even a private railway to carry the lime to the main road."

Roger shook his head in disbelief.

"Tell you what," he said suddenly. "Lime's making such a comeback. Why don't you let me take a sample of the rock away with me. I could have it analysed quite cheaply; in fact, it wouldn't cost you anything." '

"Thanks awfully," murmured Bill.

"If it's high-quality, you might be sitting on a lot of money. The farmers can't get enough of it."

"Can't get enough lime?" Bill could hardly believe his ears.

"That's right; it's used as fertiliser; ask any farmer. I'm surprised nobody's been to see you."

"I don't suppose anyone realises that it's here," replied Bill.

"Well, I'm not joking, old boy. You'll see."

Roger Bancroft's visit to Barmoor marked a turning point in Bill's life. It was also a prelude to the creeping disaster about to overtake the Sitwell home and the lands surrounding it. Yet, Bill did have a sense of premonition. Through his father's books, he knew a good deal of local history: in 1613 Lord Walden had unroofed Lindisfarne, removing the bells, the lead, and anything of value, but the ship that carried these spoils sank with all hands. Then too, there were the garrisons under siege who, having eaten all their horses and with no food left but themselves, surrendered. No, I don't need a warning, Bill thought: this corner of the world was his, and his alone now

THE FAMILY

BILL

My mother went to great pains to tell me how little money our family had, now that Deedle was no longer alive. The winter after he died, I was sent to stay with my cousins, the Gladstones, who lived in Dumfriesshire. Capenoch, their house, made me feel like the poorest relation. I was sixteen and relied on my mother for pocket-money. Having none of my own, I also looked to her to provide me with clothes.

For the visit, a new dinner jacket was out of the question. My father's old one would have to do; Miss Venning, our governess, who had reappeared on the scene, could easily alter it! The result was comical but it was I who had to wear it, and all I could do was suffer in silence.

David and Jim, two of the four Gladstone children, were more or less the same age as myself. Both had gone to Eton but we'd been at the same prep school, West Downs, and got along very well. Yet I dreaded the evenings when it was time to change for dinner. Shabby as I was, I made up my mind never to go and stay anywhere again, if I could avoid it. Nonetheless, a more humiliating incident was still to take place.

Sir Hugh Gladstone, my uncle, was very proud of his shoot, and rightly so. An excellent shot, he spared no pains in seeing to it that everything went like clockwork for his guests from neighbouring estates who bought their own dogs and loaders. David, Jim and I, being much younger, were told what to do and where to stand so that we'd have fairly easy shots at the driven birds. And all went smoothly until the shoot was over. I'd done quite well despite my nervousness, but when the time came to tip the gamekeeper, I found I'd only a shilling in the pocket of my worn plus fours. The sour look on the man's face as he took the coin worried me for years. Never again, I thought.

With my father dying when he did, there'd been no one to tell me about tipping keepers; my mother had given me five shillings for the butler and a few coins extra only for emergencies. I was ill-equipped to visit a place like Capenoch. I could shoot and should have known how to behave and the ways of the hunt, but I didn't.

I suppose, my life would've been different had my father lived. I didn't dislike my time at Harrow, I quite enjoyed it and made good friends. I was my best at games and ended up a monitor with all the privileges that went with it, but I had no monitor of my own.

It was when the holidays started that I became unhappy and bored and oddly distressed. It seemed as though my mother had lost interest in her own children, except for Simon.

I'd a great friend at Harrow called Brian Burletson whose father was something to do with shipping. At seventeen I asked if Brian could approach his father to arrange a trip on a company ship, colliers which traded out of Newcastle. By the time the summer holidays arrived, I was able to go to sea, thanks to old Burletson.

I wasn't at Barmoor much after that.

Whenever I asked if a friend could come to stay, a reason was produced for putting the visit off until later; so I gave up asking. Admittedly, some of the people my mother invited to Barmoor weren't too bad and things improved the summer before the War. Ann was married by then. I was twenty-three and up at Oxford.

It was those years after Deedle died which I shall never forget. Unfortunately, they were just the years, when what one did and how one behaved influenced one's later life so much.

My financial situation improved dramatically when I reached twenty-one. My trusts became operative, I felt quite well off. At a garden party at Barmoor on my birthday, the estate workers gave me a clock. Back at Oxford, I'd a car and a fine allowance.

But still I felt a misfit. Not all the time, but whenever I was with people of my own background: those who lived in the country, went salmon fishing, hunted and were good shots. They, of course, regarded me as an absolute crank. "D'you know about that chap Bill Sitwell?"

"Can't say I do."

"Well, he lives in a castle in Northumberland, a beautiful place, I'm told, and all he ever does with himself is push off in dirty old tramp steamers."

"Must be border-line mad, dear chap."

Well, perhaps I was a bit mad; but at least I was happy then. I loved those unkempt ships, and, for an unaccountable reason, the crews on board accepted me; I never felt at all awkward or conscious of my background, because I'd spent so much of my boyhood playing with the Thomson children at Barmoor.

During the thirties, shipping was at its lowest ebb. Hundreds were laid up in port, and there were queues down at the Milldam at South Shields, of seamen looking for work.

I was never actually signed on like the others but was taken as a supernumerary; not that it made any difference, I stood watches with the men as well. After a time I got my discharge book; my voyages were entered in it and verified by the ship's master.

1936 was the year I shan't forget. Several ships were lost in the North Atlantic, including the *Millpool* owned by Ropner's. I'd a close shave that winter also. There was the *Sheafbrook* whose owners were a Newcastle firm called W.A.Souter. The trip after I left her, she went down with all hands in the North Sea. It was bad weather, that must have caused her cargo of coal to shift, or she had her wooden hatch covers stoved in by the heavy sea.

Yet I spent as much time as I could on the colliers but was never able to stay with them for long as I was still at Harrow; later on when I was at Oxford, I regularly took Simon from Newcastle to London by sea.

The single fare on the passenger service from Newcastle Quay to Free Trade wharf was 15 shillings, and food, or victualling as it was called, was an extra 7 shillings and sixpence. Simon's first trip was in the *Newminster* owned by Tyne-Tees Shipping. He was seasick at first but recovered enough to spend practically the whole trip in the engine-room watching the machinery. I preferred to be on deck, although I'd served as a fireman and trimmer any number of times when I was in the colliers.

I didn't mind being thought an eccentricity by Northumbrians; they only shrugged their shoulders and continued on to enjoy their country pursuits. The few girls I came across were quite intrigued by me, I suspect. In any case, I had good stories, all true. One of my forearms held a long deep scar, the result of a fierce knife fight with a crew off a ship in Gdynia, Poland, where I crewed a collier called the *Aydon*. We had all been to the cinema; a bunch of men sitting in front of us kicked up a racket and wouldn't quiet down when we asked them to. The fight outside the cinema was inconclusive, so later on, when we were all turned in, asleep in the foc'c's'tle, they slipped aboard and attacked us in our bunks. I was lucky to live.

The "Bill's a tough guy" image stuck with me. My friends at Oxford found me an original sort; they'd never come across any-one like me! My reputation for living dangerously grew so tall, people thought I was engaged in gun-running with "Potato Jones", a master of a Jack Billmeir coaster who achieved fame by carrying cargoes of food, potatoes too, to the starving Spanish insurgents in Santander and other ports not occupied by General Franco.

I rather liked this image; it madé it easier when the moment arrived, not infrequently, to confess that I didn't, and couldn't play tennis or, for that matter, bridge, let alone dance or ride a horse or tie a fly. In fact, I was unable to do any of the things expected of the owner of a castle and several thousand acres.

The only kindred soul I knew with similar inadequacies, was Roddie Lambton, who spent a lot of time at Fenton, the next door estate to Barmoor. He was a delightful person whom we all loved but, sadly, he died young, the year the War started.

I got on better with my mother as I became older. We had a like sense of humour; it amused me the way she could mimic people. I read geography at Oxford and to help with my thesis, I went to South America for first hand experience. My mother decided to come with me: she was writing a book about wild flowers. I began to see her in quite a different light and forgave her for taking so little trouble over me after my father died. However, I was not amused having to listen to her carrying on about her darling Simon. He actually appeared in her worst book, a novel, after he ran away from Barmoor on his 16th birthday.

I remember his goodby note very well: I found it when I came down to breakfast one morning. He'd had a letter telling him that he'd passed his school certificate exam but this didn't deter him from biking to Newcastle, intent on following my example and signing on to a ship. His sudden departure caused a lot of alarm, but the next day he reappeared, having spent a wet, uncomfortable night on Newcastle town moor where he had pitched a little tent. He wasn't punished otherwise. He could do no wrong; not for long anyway. He always seemed to get his way and could twist my mother round his littlest finger.

For a year before the War, after he left Harrow at seventeen, we became much closer. We'd walk for hours up and down the East drive discussing the family. It was nice to have somebody to talk to; he knew quite a lot about ships. I managed to get him a trip in one old tramp, the *Carslogie* of Glasgow, when he was undecided what to do and couldn't face the idea of another spell at a crammer in London. He only wanted to go to sea then. He'd failed to get into the Navy and wasn't keen to go into the Army; not for a time anyway. To keep the pot boiling, as it were, he joined the Territorial battalion. I understood too well his wish to get away from Barmoor.

I told him what to do and, sure enough, he took himself off to Surrey docks in London. He waited for a ship, due to dock, and after the crew were paid off, managed to get himself signed on as mess-room boy.

Yet, I felt there was a barrier between us; he wasn't as socially inadequate as I, and everything went his way. He was extremely observant and had such a knack of getting round our mother. Once, he came home after a week away and nagged her over the fact that we only had *The Times* and the *Newcastle Journal*. He wanted her to order *Picture Post* and *The Bystander*, magazines he'd noticed lying around other people's homes. He also seemed to have a lot of self-confidence. I believe he actually paid someone to teach him to dance and he was quite a good piano player.

With the arrival of the War, everything changed though. I joined the R.N.V.R but wasn't called up until the end of 1939. Simon, on the other hand, was mobilised two or three days before War was in fact declared. He was told to report to the drill hall in the village together with the rest of the Lowick platoon. I felt very sorry for him as no one knew where they were being taken or, for that matter, when we'd ever see each other again. The soldiers didn't have any equipment to speak of, only Army issue overalls and a forage cap. A bus turned up and took the men away. The whole village turned out; it looked like a scene from *Journey's End*, with all the women weeping and throwing the men parcels of food.

Simon became a hero overnight. I got quite fed up with people asking how he was getting on and where-abouts in France he had fetched up.

It wasn't long before I was sent for too and found myself posted to the hastily armed trawlers operating out of Tynemouth.

The ships the Navy requisitioned were good enough sea boats having been middle and distant water trawlers; perfectly safe in any sort of a sea but pathetically fitted out for war. Most of them had only a couple of early Lewis guns.

Our job was to escort convoys, starting from the mouth of the Tyne, on the North-East coast, to the South coast ports, which meant going through the Straits of Dover. There was nothing un-toward about this, until France was over-run in 1940; the Germans virtually controlled the Channel waters then. Every time we went through the Straits, long-range guns at Calais shelled us while JU 87s dive-bombed us.

Emerging unscathed after a year, I was posted to corvettes, then served in a Colony class cruiser, then posted back to corvettes with my own command. So passed six extremely uncomfortable and dangerous years.

The Navy must've thought quite highly of me as they offered me a permanent commission, quite a rare thing in those days; very few "Wavy Navy" types like myself received such an offer.

I turned down the chance as I'd married Betty Campbell. She didn't like the idea of being married to a relatively junior officer.

I could see her point of view. She was ten or eleven years older than me and would've found it awkward when the officers' wives got together. Also, we both had large estates in need of running and the idea of that, after six years at sea, quite appealed to me. We lived at Lennel until the Army de-requisitioned Barmoor and my mother left for London. Betty and I planned to live in Barmoor once it was made habitable again; it all made sense to me at the time. Marrying Betty seemed very natural and inevitable. We had known each other a long time, our families were related through her first husband, George Campbell. The summer before the War, Simon and I were always over at Lennel; the mistake I made was in not realising what life in Berwickshire and north Northumberland would be like, as our unconventional ways appealed to Betty and her young sister Pussy Waring. Simon rather fancied Pussy but she was quite a lot older too and soon married someone more suitable: Eric de-la-Rue, a real countryman, both amusing and among the finest shots in the north of England. He was the sort of chap Betty was supposed to marry; perfectly happy pottering about all day with a pocketful of ferrets and extremely popular as well. When it came to an after-dinner discussion on the merits of a dog-pack versus a bitch-pack, he held his own comfortably. He seemed to know everybody. It intrigued me then and, for that matter, still does, why Old Etonians seem to know absolutely everyone while Old Harrovians, like myself, don't!

I soon felt completely out of water at Lennel. It was bad luck on Betty. She was puzzled and disappointed by my obvious inability to get along with her friends. I'd sit through a dinner party, hardly able to open my mouth, afraid to make some frightful gaffe. The men sat for ages after the meal, drinking port and talking about their hunting exploits and the prospects for the next grouse season. Admittedly most of them had done their stuff in the War and were nice enough individually.

I knew then, as I'd always known, I was the misfit; even being the owner of a castle didn't appeal to me. Nothing could've induced me to take up farming or forestry or anything to do with the land. I still ask myself what the hell does interest me; I still don't know.

Good Betty did her best to make me feel at ease. We'd a child together, a little girl but she only lived a day or so. Doctors weren't well equipped then for problems such as Rhesus factors.

Eventually I got so fed up with life at Lennel, I went to Iceland on the chance of a ship-delivery job. Betty came with me and for a time I felt my old self again; however, Betty was friendly with the British Minister and his wife, who often invited us to dinner and that sort of thing. I was happier spending an evening at the Missions to Seamen or an equally humble establishment.

In the end Betty and I drifted apart. She went home to Lennel and I to Guernsey on some pretext or other; we both realised that we'd made a mistake; not that we ever sat down and talked about our marriage. I've never been good at personal conversations; they embarrass me and I'm soon out-argued by strong women like Betty especially. She wasn't to blame for the failure of the marriage; how was she to know that I'd become the morose, boring, and bad-tempered man I clearly was to her friends? I never made her understand why I was like I was; I didn't know the answer myself then, though it's clear enough now.

I'd quite a good time in Guernsey. An old Harrovian lived there. I soon met other nice people. One persuaded me to invest in a shipping venture. It was a disaster. I lost all my money. I realised, I lacked something very important; the ability to say 'No' to any sort of request. I've never understood why; it's a character flaw. I'm far too obliging and helpful! It doesn't matter if it's a question of guaranteeing somebody's overdraft or lending hard cash, I've never learned my lesson. I'm too easy a touch, as the saying goes.

I once asked Simon, on one of our walks up and down the East drive at Barmoor, if he suffered from the same thing. "I wish I just wasn't so damned helpful, when it comes to money," I said.

"How d'you mean that?"

"I invariably offer an answer to please the other person, not to something outrageous but to ordinary requests, like helping someone who's got himself into a mess. Is it because I never had proper business training, thanks to that bloody War?"

Simon nodded. "West Downs has a lot to do with it," he said.

"West Downs?"

"Yes. A marvellous school, but it didn't equip us for reality. We spent far too much time in chapel, and on Mr Tindall's principles, the honesty, bravery and purity thing. Very commendable but it caused us to be too polite. In every attempt to be well-mannered, we end up agreeing badly, against our better judgment."

"I know," I said.

"It doesn't take long to regret it. I've often cursed myself after-wards for being so polite."

"You don't think it has more to do with our upbringing?"

"I don't think so. I mean, we do have the same parents."

"But you've never done some of the stupid things I have."

"I almost have," he answered. "In Johannesburg I nearly bought a garage; it seemed a wonderful idea at the time but as luck would have it, I couldn't raise the money."

"I made a bloody fool of myself in the Channel Islands over the *Dames des I'sles*," I said.

"Yes, I heard about that. Bad news travels faster than good."

"I didn't know you were interested in African garages," I said.

"I'm not! I met a man who wanted to retire. He convinced me his was a wonderful business; it'd make me rich."

"Was that true?"

"Of course not. He turned out to be a con man. I should have listened to our father's territorial rules."

"Deedle didn't have to die on us," I said. "He smoked his way to death. That was a worse mistake. I think I resent him for it."

For a long while I wasn't living anywhere permanently, though I came back to Barmoor from time to time. There wasn't a great deal to do. Most of my money had been lost; to make a bit I did ship-delivery work but only sporadically. Arriving in Copenhagen, I met Anna. We hit it off from the word go and she moved in with me to stay at Barmoor.

Simon didn't like that. He tried to talk her into leaving, to live in Newcastle; somewhere not so close to Betty. I started to openly dislike him then, the sanctimonious little sod. It wasn't that he was conceited or unpleasant, but I was jealous that he always seemed to come off better. Take the War; he ended up a bloody hero with a D.F.C. and Christ knows what! He had an important job in the City and was the apple of our mother's eye, but that didn't give him the right to come up to Barmoor and interfere over things which were nothing to do with him. He had guts, mind you and did not care who he took on. The way he'd gone over to Lennel and got back my suits; he even told the old girl about Anna's baby! I could never have brought myself to do that.

It didn't take me long to get fed up with Anna either. Summer time wasn't too bad, because Ann came to stay and once or twice Simon's wife brought her children up. They loved the place and thought it beautiful. No one could deny that; but living there year-round was quite a different matter.

Anna started drinking; nothing serious but it was noticeable, especially in the evenings. I can't say I blame her; I wasn't very good company and frankly didn't much like making conversation after a day spent in Newcastle at Harrison and Shipley's office. The journey took an hour and a half each way. I was pretty tired by the time I got home.

Even then, Simon had to poke his nose in. "D'you mean to tell me they're not paying you a thing?" he asked on one of his visits.

"Not for the time being."

"Why don't you talk to them? Find out what they've in mind."

'I wish to Christ he'd lay off hectoring me,' I thought. 'It's none of his bloody business, but I suppose he thinks he knows it all, just because he's working for Clarksons.'

"You can't expect them to pay me while I'm still being trained," I said.

"Why not?" he asked.

"I'm no use to them yet. I'm no more than an office boy."

"Thats what you think. I'm sure they're very pleased with you. Look at the way you shifted that ship to a new berth yesterday. You told me you did it almost single handed."

"Alright, let's not argue about it. I'll talk to them."

Instead I gave up going to Newcastle. The partners in Harrison & Shipley had hinted that they were looking around for another ship and wanted a working partner, who could put up the money. They didn't know, that I'd lost everything in Guernsey. I told them instead, I intended to spend more of my time at Barmoor and did not think it worth my while carrying on; so that was that!

I was very hard up then, since I had to send money to Anna for herself and the boy. However as luck would have it, I bumped into to a little man I knew vaguely from the village pub. He asked if I'd be interested in selling timber to the National Coal Board, cut to a special size. We had the equipment for the job on the estate and soon I'd a thriving little business going and was sending lorry loads of the stuff off every week. Most of it went to a pit in the south of the county, to Embleton colliery.

By selling a few of the better paintings in the house, I amassed extra capital and, for a time, quite enjoyed life. It helped to avoid most of my neighbours. Friends I'd made in Newcastle came to spend weekends; business people, they didn't sit over their port for hour after hour talking about their horses and grouse moors.

On my own, I'd sit by the fire in the dining-room at Barmoor and think about my ancestors. They'd been a hard living lot! The fireplace was circular and could be rotated to reveal a second grate. My father told me that he and his friends often sat up so long at night that the servants hardly had time to lay and light a new fire, between the time the men went to bed and reappeared for an early hunting breakfast. I wonder what they would've made of me, as what I detested more than anything else was horses. And yet, a hundred years ago, my great-grandfather devoted all his time to his hounds and being an outstanding horseman. One only had to look at the stables at Barmoor to understand how he spent away his money. I was not going to do the same.

I drew comfort from the fact, I was bound to be different, faced as I was with a selfish mother, who, quite inadvertently, by discouraging me, took away my self-confidence as I was growing up.

Brighton and Campbell Cotts gave it back to me. The people I met excited me. They were amusing, attractive, uninhibited, and found me interesting. For the first time since I'd been up at Oxford, I felt able to hold my own, to be able to converse free from shyness and awkwardness. After a drink or two, my personality seemed to change; I found myself relating amusing incidents; I was alive.

Campbell was never far away. He introduced me to everyone in sight. He knew very many people and everything about them. Heaven only knows what Campbell said to them where I was concerned; he was such a gossip and full of intrigue but incredibly kind and generous. Year after year, he asked my mother to attend his lavish luncheon parties in the Hyde Park Hotel. She only went to a few, finding them altogether too noisy and wild.

I could have stayed at Brighton forever, with Campbell determined to show me off, as if he'd suddenly discovered me. It was quite embarrassing at times listening to him going on about what an old family the Sitwells were. He painted an exaggerated picture, of course, how I was a restless soul, a sea captain, and a War hero, wedded to my ships but at the same time owning a stately home in the north of England. I didn't discourage him; I enjoyed being at the centre of attention and finding myself surrounded by people so unlike my Barmoor neighbors; to Campbell and his friends, hunting and shooting were subjects people made jokes about.

Then I met Penelope. She swept me up completely. This witty, beautiful creature, the darling of Broadway and one of England's best known actresses responding to me, I found it hard to believe! A social misfit such as I, with nearly no money, to be adored by Penelope; it was almost a fairy story.

Her first visit to Barmoor was a great success. I shudder to think what I spent but I wasn't feeling hard up at the time as the sawmills were doing so well and I had endless trees to cut down. I drove into Berwick and bought enormous quantities of drink and the sort of rich food my party enjoyed.

Penelope's was such a different world to the one I was used to. The jokes and the stories, her sophisticated casual approach and her apparent boredom with the usual upper class country pursuits elevated me. My morale and self-confidence, never very high but lower than ever after two unsuccessful marriages, soared as the days went past; I insisted that she come and stay again.

A terrible sense of anti-climax came over me after her visits however. I knew that I couldn't keep the pace up for long; the tradesmen's bills made that quite clear. One day I'd have to put a stop to this madness, but not yet. Why shouldn't I enjoy life for a change? It hadn't been much fun until now. I deserved a good time after those God-awful, dangerous, tedious years of war.

On numerous occasions I was on my own, in the evenings, and

the reality of life would strike me. Who was I, what was I doing with myself, and what on earth would I do in future? Already, I was responsible for a wife and son; two wives, come to think of it, if I included Betty! But she never asked for a thing; she was gone from my life forever. It would've surprised me if she even knew where I was; our paths never crossed, her friends and mine didn't know one another.

'Where the hell am I going?' I'd ask myself as I stared into the fire with the double grate. Newcastle was hopeless without money.

Simon spotted what was happening though and tried to persuade me to stop cutting the forests. Again he could not, and would not, mind his own business. Just because he'd been born at Barmoor, I suppose he thought it gave him the right to interfere, the bloody little nosey-parker.

When he visited, we'd still go for walks up and down the East drive and chat away but it wasn't like the old days. He disapproved of everything I was doing; or rather, not doing. And he annoyed me with his tales of city life. Not that he was showing off; quite the opposite. He was very tactful and modest, yet he was always in a hurry; invariably on his way back from Norway, or he'd be in the north of England having talks with a shipyard on the Tyne or the Clyde. And he had those war medals for his aerial marksmanship.

"Are you sure you're right about cutting down Dunsall Wood?" he asked in his best diplomatic style.

"Yes," I answered. "They're starting to go back."

"Timber takes a long time to grow," he continued.

"Yes, I know. But it's no good leaving it, it'll only go back."

"What does he mean; go back?" asked Simon. I was in the habit of using expressions the locals understood. Simon hated it when I put on a north country accent. I'd be chatting to somebody in a pub like the Black Bull at Lowick and use words like "aye" and "canny" and know Simon was thinking, Can't he just be himself?

"What d'you mean, go back?" persisted Simon.

"The trees are mature; they need felling, they're fully grown."

"Well, I suppose it's alright if you replant afterwards."

"I am replanting."

"You damned liar," Simon muttered under his breath. It very clearly annoyed him to be taken for an idiot.

"Any other questions?" I asked sarcastically, giving him a sideways glance.

"Oh, it's none of my business," he replied innocently. "It's just that I don't like seeing trees cut for no reason."

"Well, I wouldn't be cutting them if it wasn't time to do it."

'I don't suppose he believes a word I'm saying!' I thought.

We walked on with nothing much left to say.

My mother came to stay sometimes; she never brought anyone with her and didn't appear anxious to call on any of the few friends she still had in the North. She liked best to go for a drive after tea; to Bamburgh or Norham. Quite apart from their place in history, she loved the setting and situation of those old castles. Norham was a bit close to Lennel from my point of view, but I did enjoy taking her to Lindisfarne and Bewick Law.

"D'you ever see Betty?" she asked. "Beastly woman! I hope that creeper grows up again."

The creeper had enveloped Ma's bedroom window for years. Betty cut it down shortly after we'd married. Ma never forgave her!

"Look how bare it's made the house look!" she added.

I grunted. Every time Ma came to stay, she harped on the subject of the creeper. Even to my unartistic eye, it was beautiful once; a deep red, unlike the other stuff covering the rest of the house.

"What an odious woman," Ma continued.

I thought she was going to stamp her foot with rage.

"Oh, Betty wasn't as bad as all that," I said.

"What a pity you married her. I always wanted you to marry Ann Hotham."

'What's the good of saying that now,' I thought. 'Fat chance I have of marrying Ann Hotham or anyone else here. Thanks to you, largely, I never got to meet anyone my own age.'

"You didn't seem to mind Betty," I replied. "You encouraged Simon and I to go to Lennel, whenever we could."

"That was different. You just helped them move furniture."

"We did? Well, there's no point our going on about it, " I said finally. "It was a mistake and that's all there is to it."

"I never met anybody who liked Betty; or her mother, come to that," Ma said, determined still to provoke me.

"I didn't think you had friends in common," I said acidly.

"Yes, we did. The Spears took the house at Salcombe, because they couldn't bear Lady Clemmie."

'Now she's just being bloody unreasonable,' I thought. I always liked Betty's mother.

My mother returned to London, laden with flowers from the garden, and I had a letter from Roger Bancroft, a chap I'd been up at Oxford with, who worked in Johannesburg as a geologist now but was in England on holiday. He came, stayed for a few days and took away a sample from the old lime quarry, though I didn't see how he could be such an authority; after all, he'd spent his life so far only doing assay tests for South African gold producers.

I heard nothing and assumed his tests had shown the Barmoor lime to be of poor quality. I felt downcast, as I'd taken the trouble to find out how very much in demand the stuff was. I thought, 'How amazing it'd be if the quarry were resurrected. History might repeat itself; my problems would evaporate.'

Weeks passed until one day, at teatime, the telephone rang. It was the G.P.O. with a telegram. "Delighted to inform you. Tests on rock sample reveal excellent quality, suitable for fertiliser."

I put the receiver down. My hand was trembling.

I wasn't as well-suited to the savage control of the early Borderlands as I thought I'd have been..

Campbell Cotts

SIMON

IT CAN'T HAVE BEEN until I was six years old, that I realised how devoted my mother was to me. Ann and Bill had gone to school and various governesses were teaching me to read and write. One was a fat Swiss lady I called Mademoiselle; I believe her real name was Frau Wengy, but no matter. She was large and comfortable and taught me a bit of French. I recall Miss Venning too, the opposite of Mademoiselle. A diminutive little creature with a long, sad face and a mournful voice. She'd reminisce, for what seemed like hours, about the period in her life that she'd spent in India.

"Yes," she'd say; "There was a time when Colonel Shires asked me whether I'd mind taking the children up to the hill station on my own; his memsahib wasn't up to the journey." She'd stop while she picked up a dropped stitch on the jersey she was knitting me. "We were at Katmandu; a beautiful place that was. Oh yes, I liked it very much. All the young officers talked to me and asked after your brother and sister. And your father; I remember once..." And Miss V, as I called her, would ramble on. Since Miss V mentioned the Shires nearly every day I wondered a lot about them. 'Fancy having Showers for a name!' I'd think.

With Ann and Bill at school and no doubt finding Barmoor rather quiet and empty, my mother spent much time with me. We adored each other; in winter she played with me after tea in front of the fire in the green drawing-room; during summer, we went for walks together looking for mushrooms. On the last day before we went back to the London house, we invariably prepared a picnic tea and carried it to a place down at the quarry. Always the same place, year after year, on a ledge, where we'd spread a rug and have our meal. Flocks of seagulls, having followed the plough all day, flew eastwards toward the sea, returning to Holy Island or the Outer Farnes less than ten miles away.

Perhaps my mother found me more sensitive than her other children; more responsive and affectionate then. My sister Ann was eight years older than I. So far as I was concerned, she was a scatter-brained idiot who was a spoil-sport, forever losing things.

It wasn't until many years later that we were able to talk to each other properly.

Bill was four years older than I. Someone must've told him to break the sad news to me that my father was dying. I remember perfectly; we were up at the shacks in Dunsall Wood when he broached the subject. I must've been preoccupied; I didn't take it in. I've often thought about that since. I must've nodded my head or given him some indication that I understood, because the inevitable wasn't mentioned again. I was distraught with grief when my father did die. I desperately wanted one last look at him but wasn't allowed. Even now, I feel guilty that I didn't sit with him on his last day. A West Downs friend had come to Barmoor; we were so absorbed with our bicycles that I never went to see my father on his death-bed. To this day, I fearfully imagine his face, unlined and calm, lying in his room with the blinds drawn, waiting for the undertakers to prepare him for his last journey to Lowick church.

Everything changed then. There was some doubt as to whether I could stay on at West Downs. My mother was obsessed by our poverty. She wrote to Mr Tindall, the headmaster, asking if he could reduce the fees. I'm sure that her cry for help did not go unheeded. I remained at school till my time to move on to Harrow.

In contrast to my happy years at West Downs, I'd a wretched time at Harrow, thanks to a thoroughly idle house-master who preferred to sit over his port rather than counsel with the boys he had charge of. I was bullied and badly taught. More out of self-defence than anything else, I took up boxing and made the school team. After dealing with my chief tormentor in time-honoured fashion, a challenge with bare fists in the common-room in front of an audience, I was left in peace and quite enjoyed my last year.

While at Harrow, I started to copy my brother and spend more and more time at sea. There was nothing at all to do at Barmoor except for bicycle rides and playing with the Thomson boys. I did manage to assemble a small workshop in an unused room at the bottom of the house, where I made engine models; unfortunately my skills were hampered by a complete lack of funds.

After Harrow, I spent a summer on a Baltic island, hoping the

change would help me decide what to do. It was a waste of time;
I returned home still undecided. Against my mother's wishes, I
signed on a tramp steamer, the 6347 ton, 5/5 *Carslogie* owned by
Messrs. Honeyman Brothers of Hope Street, Glasgow. On a gusty
day in mid-October 1938, she sailed in ballast out of the London
river (the Thames) bound for Amsterdam.

The *Carslogie* was known as a "monthly" boat; one was paid by
the month and kept and fed by the Company. My wages were £1 a
week and "all found," a sinister term meaning I was to be provided
with the requisite food laid down by Board of Trade regulations
and given a bunk on which to rest after a twelve-hour day. I was a
privileged member of the crew in that my cabin was 'midships, not
in the fo'c'sle. I shared it with the cabin-boy, a fourteen-year old
from Cardiff; whose parents were from a Caribbean island.

The *Carslogie* was what she looked; a hard-case tramp and I, a
student of Harrow school a few months earlier, wondered if my
thirst for adventure, my determination to experience the seamy
side of life, wouldn't prove too much for me.

The ship remained at Amsterdam a short time, only enough
to have her bottom scraped and her bunkers filled with cheap
Continental coal. Then, with her holds still empty, she sailed for
the German port of Emden.

We then left there on the afternoon tide bound for Montreal. It
was blowing hard, and the equinoctial gales still had to be faced.
We steamed up the estuary to meet the North Sea. The crew went
round inspecting the hatch covers under which lay a full cargo of
anthracite. This was the last chance we'd have of walking the decks
without getting wet while clutching the life-lines. The first vicious
wave soon would slip over the bulwark onto the well-deck. I stood
in the shelter of the 'midships structure and looked out over the
flat land flanking the estuary. On the horizon a difference between
land and sky was hard to tell; both were without colour. The water
was a muddy brown and whipped up into small waves, which
slapped harmlessly against the sides of the ship; heavy, solid and
cumbersome, as we'd loaded to the international load-line; the
shallow waters did no more than float us, the ship was as yet,

steady and dry. Not so the dredgers we passed. With smoke from their funnels whipped flat by the rising wind, they groaned and clattered as they worked, the lighters alongside them bumping and pitching. The rasping squeak of the dredgers was the last loud sound outside that I was to hear until we picked up the pilot at Three Rivers a month later.

My time in the *Carslogie* taught me a lot about myself. I was only eighteen years old but resourceful and strong and could look after myself. It's often argued that some with upper-class back-grounds find it easier to form friendships with those from lower societal levels. I'm well aware. However, I genuinely liked the men I'd chosen to meet through my confused desire to see how "the other half" lived.

Bob Willis, the steward on the *Carslogie* was a case in point. He was the "old man's" confidant. The "old man", or master of the ship was Jimmy Gentiles; but ask any member of the crew who was the most feared man there and he'd name Bob.

We were in mid-Atlantic and took a big sea amidships. I spent much of my time in the engine-room and was down there when I noticed the second engineer, supposedly on watch, disappear through the alley-way connecting the engine-room with the stoke-hold. "Hey, Sammy," he yelled back. "Nip through and keep up steam; those bloody wog firemen aren't there."

As everyone called me Sammy, I did what I was told, since the necessity was soon apparent. The plates of the stokehold were running in water; from far above, a sea had flooded the fiddley grating, gaining access to the heart of the ship. It was only the eight furnaces serving the two Scotch boilers that stood between our ship's survival and the alternative. If the fires went out, there'd be no steam, the engines would stop, and the ship would quickly be overwhelmed by the raging Atlantic storm.

An hour later, things were back to normal. The steam pressure edged up to 180 pounds per square inch and the two Arab firemen reappeared. Exhausted by pitching, raking, and slicing the fires, I retired to the back of the engine-room to wash the sweat and coal dust off my body. The only hot water available was to be found in the hot well at the back of the huge triple-expansion engine which dominated the room.

I made my way to the galley half expecting a hero's welcome. There I found Bob Willis; Sparks, the wireless operator; Taffy, the cook; and the third mate, unaware of the little drama that had taken place down below.

Bob sat on top of the coal bunker holding forth. "Aye," he said. "The wireless told us that the *Cromer* lifeboat picked them up. Lot of women and children there were on that ship too. D'you mind her, Sam?" he asked, addressing me.

I remembered that ship very well. She'd been berthed near us in Surrey docks and caused quite a stir as she'd a gun mounted on her deck aft. Owned by the Spanish insurgents, she was intercepted off the English coast by a Spanish government warship. People living near the Norfolk coast heard the attacking gunfire; not since the end of the Great War, twenty years before, had there been anything like it.

"Yes," I answered. "Big grey ship, wasn't she? Registered in San Sebastian; on her way to Methil for bunkers when she went down in the end."

"Aye, likely," put in Sparks.

"It's a wonder, you know," said Bob Willis. "Now wouldn't you have thought she'd put up a fight? I mean to say, she had a big gun on her poop, from what I remember of her. Now what would you have done, Sam?" and he winked at the others.

There was a silence.

"Now come on," he persisted. " Tell us what you would've done if she'd been your ship. Would you have taken to the boats or would you have fought?"

Bob loved to pull my leg, often by asking for my opinion.

"I'd have tried beaching her," I answered.

"Now Sam," Bob wagged a finger at me and looked serious. "I think you've got something there, lad."

And so the conversation drifted on while outside the gale piled the great waves higher and higher, but I'd done my part. We were all safe and at ease.

After three months in the *Carslogie* I paid off in Ardrossan and went home to Barmoor. But not for long. I was soon back at sea but not for such a lengthy voyage.

As a concession to my mother and because it was time I made a decision on a career, and in memory of my father, I agreed to go into the Army as a regular soldier. I'd left it too late to go to Sandhurst or Woolwich. To gain a commission, it was necessary to join the Territorial Army and then, after a spell at University, I could be posted to the regiment of my choice.

Having already passed the required entrance exams, it was arranged that I go up to Oxford in the autumn of 1939. I'd have preferred to enter the Navy or, better still, be an engineer in the Merchant Service. With all the talk of a European war, I signed with the Merchant War Service a few days before I presented myself at the recruiting office of the Northumberland Fusiliers. If there is to be a war, I thought, I'll be able to get back to sea; by then, I had my discharge book, the equivalent of a seaman's passport. I was even a member of the National Union.

Days before war was declared, my dreams were abruptly put to an end: I was told to go to Lowick drill hall. Other members of the village platoon appeared; after an emotional hour of farewells, a bus arrived and took us away into Berwick. No one knew where we were going; it was a bit of an anti-climax to be deposited soon after, on the steps of the Berwick Company headquarters of the 7th battalion, the "Fighting Fifth".

I spent the first two years of the War in the Army and rose up through the ranks to become an officer, but, in frustration, wasted far too much time wondering how to transfer on to the Merchant Service. I saw various senior officers and explained that marine engineers were in short supply and I ought to be released. My pleas and arguments fell on deaf ears; to make matters worse, I was not allowed to serve overseas as regulations prohibited staff under 21 from being posted abroad. It looked as if I'd be condemned forever to being a machine-gun instructor in Newcastle.

But luck was on my side, as I happened to be passing a notice board and stopped to glance at an Army Council Instruction which said that officers physically fit and proficient at Morse code, or Wireless Telegraphy, could apply for secondment to the Air Force. A shortage of pilots for Army co-operation work needed to be addressed.

After two weeks training on the Morse key and the Aldis lamp, I qualified with the necessary speed. Next was a transfer to the Air Force. I was given a very stiff medical in London and an even stiffer eyesight test, but passed both. Six months later though, I'd given up hope of anything happening, when suddenly I was ordered to report to an airfield in the South of England.

I'd seen very little of my brother and sister up until then but we managed a few days together in Bristol where Bill was standing by a ship being built there. I didn't tell my mother I was training to be a pilot. It seemed pointless when I might not even qualify.

After a hundred hours flying Tiger Moths, I was posted to Cranwell for the next part of the programme on a more sophisticated machine called a Miles Master, with an enclosed cockpit, retractable undercarriage and a powerful radial engine. To sit in a warm cockpit after the open ones of the elementary trainers was a great luxury. Most of the pilots got through the course without too much trouble. And eight months after leaving the Army, the great day arrived when my name was called and a senior officer from the Air Ministry, who'd come to Cranwell for the occasion, pinned the pilot's brevet onto my chest.

After another course, to familiarise myself with American aircraft, I was posted to 613 Squadron, City of Manchester. They'd been flying Lysanders and Tomahawks but had just received the first of the American lease-lend planes, the P-51 pursuit attacker, commonly known as a Mustang. It was a thoroughbred fighter, sleek and long-nosed. Before we were allowed to fly one, we spent hours doing cockpit drill, till we were able to recite all the vital actions and desired readings before take-off. I'll never forget the first time I took one up. Until then, the aircraft I'd flown were dual-equipped: an instructor could take over should I lose control or get into a danger. "Alright, Sitwell; go down to the tent, get your lunch, and you can fly directly after," I heard, finally.

"Gussy" Sheret and Brian Slack, trainee pilots like myself, ate a silent meal together. In an hour, we'd fly our first single-seater aeroplane: a real fighter and an unpleasant prospect.

Trim - mixture - pitch - fuel - flaps - radiator - tailwheel lock - hydraulics, I muttered to myself as I taxied. Vital actions before take-off.

A few minutes later I was flying down the road from Oatlands Hill to Salisbury. How smooth she was. Like being in a Packard after a Morris 8. After ten minutes, I readied for my first landing. Throttle back, 10 degrees of flap to get the speed down, radiator a quarter open, then lower the undercarriage.

That evening, in the "Haunch of Venison" with friends, I asked Bill Bodington, "Tell me, old boy, what's that peculiar noise I hear when I lower the under-cart?'

"Oh, I forgot to warn you. They all make that noise, nothing to worry about."

"It gave me the most awful fright; I thought the whole kite was falling to bits."

"Well, what d'you think of them now that you've soloed?"

"Absolutely wizard," I said.

After flying fighters for two years, my squadron re-equipped with fighter-bombers and most operations were now carried out in the dark. Hour after hour was spent in the mess waiting to hear whether or not there'd be an op that night. Most of the crews sat around reading old newspapers or playing endless games of shove ha'penny. We weren't allowed off the station if we were on battle order, the list pinned up in the mess detailing which crews were on stand-by to be briefed for ops. And there was no drinking.

The squadron was next sent to an airfield called Wellingore, not far from Grantham and conveniently near the East coast. Each pilot had his own aircraft and flew it alone. My Mustang was called *Grey County*; my rigger painted the Northumberland County's coat of arms on the engine cowling. Each morning, my AP-207 was groomed, just like a thoroughbred. Leading Aircraftsman Claxton, who hailed from Norwich, worked hard on the hood with perspex cleaner; someone else in the ground crew worked on the leading edge and spinner with smooth-grained emery paper; anything to get a few extra miles per hour of speed.

At dawn each day two of us went up to the airfield to warm up the aircraft, in the event of being scrambled. We'd sit then in the flight office, huddled up in our Irvine jackets. From time to time, we'd go outside to look at the weather, and then go back into the office to wait and wonder whether the telephone would ring and order us to get airborne. Hours of boredom passed with a bit of fear and anxiousness mixed in.

My first real sadness was when Harry Sackville went missing. On 15th May 1943, he and Tim Dooley, his New Zealand flight commander, took off on a shipping reconnaissance over the Frisian Islands. They didn't return. It was our first casualty since Alred Usher-Smith ditched his aircraft off Beachy Head the winter before, coming back from a "rhubarb" over France.

I had been on the same op and watched it happen.

No one saw Usher again.

It took Bill Bodington a long time to recover from Harry's disappearance; he was a close friend to him; so was I for that matter. Later on in the War, while I was flying Mosquitos, the casualty rate was tremendous but, in those days in Lincolnshire, we were a much smaller squadron and not hardened to losing our best.

Perhaps the first real flying shock was about 1st May that year, a fortnight before Harry and Tim went missing. We provided rear cover for a medium-level raid on an Amsterdam power station, coupled with a diversionary attack on the coke-oven plant at the mouth of the North Sea canal. I couldn't help remembering how often I'd carried coking coal to Terneuzen when I'd been at sea; it seemed like another life. This particular raid was a disaster, however, from start to finish. Of the twelve Ventura aircraft from 2 Group, that tried to bomb the power station, only one returned. The boffins who had planned the op had made a mix-up over the timing, with the result that the dreaded "den Helder" boys with their FW-190s were waiting for us when we crossed the Dutch coast. We'd been briefed to protect the six Bostons which were supposed to carry out a low level attack on the coke ovens, but it ended with every man for himself, and I made it back alone alive.

I never told my family what was going on, but my mother really didn't mind the idea of my flying. What a twist of fate it was that her darling Simon should be emulating her beloved Reggie, who flew fighters in the Great War, but it must've been frightful for her having both her sons "at the front". Yet, the fate of mothers whose husbands were killed in the Great War and their children in the Second was far worse.

"You will take care, won't you, darling?" was about as far as my mother went when we said goodbye. Sometimes she wanted me to reassure her that I believed like her in life after death; she went regularly to the London Spiritualist Alliance HQ in Queensberry Place but not so often to a medium anymore. She'd become fully involved with the Spiritualist movement and, indeed, after the War, was President of the LSA.

At the end of that year, by which time I'd done 33 daylight ops in Mustangs, the squadron moved again to an airfield at Lasham in Hampshire and was re-equipped with Mosquito MK-6 fighter-bombers. None of us had been trained to fly twin-engined aircraft and a number of crews lost their lives through accidents. Worse, the complement of aircrew in the squadron was doubled as the Mosquito carried a navigator.

Apart from a break of six weeks' leave, after I'd completed fifty more ops, mostly at night, I remained flying Mozzies, as we called them, until practically the end of the European war. I'd survived 70 sorties so far; only two other men out of the original squadron were still alive; Knight and Gardner. More than 90 crews had joined the squadron during my time with it and they'd all been killed or gone missing. It didn't bother us all that much until crews disappeared whom we knew well and had a reputation for being high skilled and experienced.

I asked myself how I could have come through alive till now, the law of averages being what it is. Admittedly, my confidence grew the more I flew and flying against targets at night eventually became preferable to attacking by daylight; I got to appreciate the night clouds which I could hide in, if pursued by an enemy fighter. I doubt, however, if any pilot ever really comes to terms with a night take-off.

For my third tour of ops, I was posted to (Polish) 305 Squadron and given a new navigator, a lieutenant in the Norwegian Air Force, from Oslo, named Ivar von Krogh. For about a month, to get used to each other, we went on ferrying duties flying transport aircraft between Hartford Bridge, in the south of England, and Brussels. We then joined the Poles in France at Epinoy, an airfield used by the Germans until the Allies over-ran it. It wasn't long before we found ourselves in our Mosquito, waiting in the darkness at the end of the runway, preparing for a night sortie.

"Chocks away, and let us pray," I whispered. "O.K, Ivar?"

"O.K," comes the reply.

"Petrol on outers?"

"On outers."

"Right - let's go."

I tighten up the throttle nut and slowly push my long levers forward. Now, the yellow needles of the boost gauges creep round the dials. Up, past nought, plus two-four-six-eight-ten, until the manifold pressure reads twelve pounds per square inch. Behind my head, the armour-plating rattles as the Merlin 25s develop full power so vital for take-off.

Tonight, the wind is down runway and there is no tendency for the Mosquito to swing. A line of yellow lights pass below and to the side, quickening until they are just a blur. My eyes are fixed on the glowing instruments in front of me. The needles of the two rev counters directly above the boost gauges have unwound them-selves but are now steady at the 3000 mark, and I breath a little more easily: 120 miles an hour shows on the air-speed indicator; there's a flash of red in the yellow lights of the runway streaking past me. The time to lift her off is now. Lift the mass of wood and glue and steel from the concrete runway. Lift over a ton of high explosive bombs, plus half a ton of ammunition, and over four hundred gallons of petrol.

"Come on, you bitch," I mutter as we come unstuck only to sink again. But seconds later we're airborne. I squeeze the brake lever before selecting "up" on the under-carriage lever. We're off!

Blackness ahead and not a trace of a horizon. My eyes don't move from the gyro and its artificial horizon. Instruments! Watch the instruments, I repeat to myself, as the altimeter needle rises reluctantly from the 400-foot mark, which I'd set before take-off, past the 1000-foot mark and through the hundreds more feet that separate us from the ground.

The undercarriage warning lights, showing dimly through the night screen, change from green to red and, as the lever jumps down to the horizontal position, go out altogether.

I listen carefully to the noise of the engines, my ears blocked by the falling air pressure, but I still hear every beat. If those Merlins so much as cough now, it's the end for my navigator on my right and me. He's already testing the Gee set, quite ignoring what's taking place a few inches to his left.

I throttle back to 7 pounds boost; feel for the knurled locking nut for the pitch levers and slacken off. Now the revs are coming back and the engines drum and beat as they fall out of synchro. Flaps up and radiators closed; two small switches below the heavy glass windscreen — I flick them up and the nose of the Mosquito drops before I trim back on the big wheel beside my left thigh.

170 mph on the clock and, as I turn, I see the flare-path lying beneath my left shoulder. We are off, off to Wessel, Munster and Osnabruck, we are off to the Ruhr.

"Onto inners, Gee alright?" I say in one breath.

"On inners; Gee's O.K." is the reply.

"Jelly two three airborne; onto channel B." I say, as I press the transmitting switch with my left forefinger.

"Roger, two three," comes the reply.

I feel for push-button studs on the little box below the engine controls. "One, two," I count, then, push the next one down. A clicking in my ears and I hear far off voices as frequencies change; now I'm listening out on the operational frequency.

At two thousand feet, I level out and bring the aircraft onto course. "On 069, angels two, 240 indicated, we're a minute and a half late," I say to Ivar.

"Near enough," he answers.

I settle down for another op. The take-off is over; the most nerve-racking part of the sortie is finished with and I'm left alone with my thoughts.

Still, I watch the instruments; the gyro, the artificial horizon, the climb and descent indicator and the airspeed. One can think and watch them automatically but thoughts intrude. Night take-offs preoccupy me. Do other pilots go through the same sweaty, concentrated hell? Am I different? I suspect not.

I remained in the Air Force for a few more years until I was de-mobilized at the end of 1945. As a pilot in an operational squadron, I had privileges not enjoyed by anyone else, with the possible exception of the men who went to sea in submarines and aircrew in the Fleet Air Arm. Many people may disagree with me but I remember those years as time wasted, an amalgam of exhilaration, boredom, sadness and fear; I experienced many more emotions but I remember the endless waiting and consequent boredom best.

BLACK STORM-CLOUDS over the Cheviots. A gale of wind blowing from the north-west; a wild, stormy evening. Slessor, the game-keeper at Lennel and I stand on a spit in the middle of the Tweed.

I've been a few days at Lennel. It's just starting to get dark and we're waiting for the duck to flight. Betty suggested I might try to get something for the larder. That afternoon, Slessor and I fished the river without success. Determined to provide for the house-hold, I suggested that we go after duck that very evening.

"And when d'you think the War'll be over, Master Simon?"

"Shouldn't be long now, Slessor."

The conversation reminded me of the one I'd had with Smith, the head gardener at Barmoor, a few days before War was declared. He was dead now, with only Thomson left.

"Aye, looks as if we've got old Jerry on the run at last," he said, his eyes scanning the sky for signs of duck.

"I rather doubt it'll be over this year," I replied, given the British set-back at Arnhem.

"They tell us you're doing a trip with Mister Bill over to Ireland."

"Yes, that's right. He's taking me from Liverpool to Belfast in his corvette. It'll be quite a change."

"Aye, a nice change from flying, doubtless. I've often wondered why you didn't follow the sea like Mister Bill."

'Little does he know how hard I tried,' I thought, but before I could think of what to tell he held up his hand.

"Psst — here they come, Master Simon. D'ye no hear them?"

Faintly, above the wind and the sound of the river, came that peculiar soft swishing sound of ducks in flight.

Sometimes I found my brother at Barmoor or Lennel on one of his rare leaves. "What about coming over to Ireland in the *Flint Castle* with me," he suggested.

As I had a few days of squadron leave left, I agreed.

All day the wind increased. By the time we reached the ship, berthed in the Gladstone dock at Liverpool, it was blowing a gale. We left the next morning at five. For'ard and aft were two tugs; it was still blowing hard, and a lovely, wild sight. I was allowed to stand in the wing of the bridge. The white beam of a searchlight lit a patch of rough water ahead. The new pilot took us out of the dock and into the Mersey. Liverpool Bay was covered with white horses, and it wasn't long before the ship buried her sharp nose in the waves. There was no sign now of the pilot boat. "She'll have run for shelter," said the old pilot. "I'll come over with you."

That evening we anchored in Bangor Bay and I left the ship.

Bill and Betty married early that year. I'd always had a warm spot for the Warings and was quite pleased; the marriage seemed a marvellous idea. Sitting in the train on my way to Belfast though, I'd the uncomfortable feeling that I'd never see Bill again. I'd had it once before, in the first winter of the war. I'd gone to North Shields just in time to see him slackening off the for'ard springs of his ship preparatory to leaving for another North Sea patrol. He was mate then of the armed trawler *Loch Oskaig*. Only the week before, the *Loch Doon*, another armed trawler, failed to return. Ships were being mined and sinking within sight of the Tyne piers.

I thought of the holidays at Barmoor after my father died. Bill had been a wonderful brother to me. Without being asked, he'd decided, whatever his own shortcomings, I'd be properly brought up. This meant being punctual, eating correctly, washing one's hands before a meal, and things like that. I never questioned his authority. If Bill said, "You're not staying in here," referring to the dining-room, "Go and stand outside," I didn't argue. I'd go and stand outside the door until, perhaps after ten minutes, it'd open and a gruff voice would say: "You can come in now; but if you don't behave, you're out again, understand?"

He'd been sixteen years old, I twelve when Deedle died; his was an extraordinary performance by a person his age, as if he was speaking for someone outside himself, Deedle perhaps, who instructed him as to what to say.

My mother backed him up. "Go and do what Bill says, darling."

I'd slink out of the room wondering if anyone remembered to put my plate, with its barely touched food, onto the hot-plate with the small methylated spirit stoves burning underneath.

The gap between Bill and I shrunk quite rapidly as I became older. Even before the War, when I was sixteen, we'd talk for hours about our experiences in the colliers. We'd compare notes on the hard case owners and the ships we'd served in. The owners who came from the North East ports found it hardest to sign a crew, as they didn't always comply with regulations. Seamen were unaware of the safeguards employed to protect them. They'd never heard of Lloyd's Register, or the Classification Societies and their regular inspections or how they measured the thickness of the plates, and the countless other tests, progressively stricter as the years went by, to ensure that no ship classified with Lloyd's should be unseaworthy.

Victualling was another bone of contention; the subject of hours of debate in pubs up and down the country where seamen congregated to squander the few pounds they'd been given when they paid off.

My brother and I were on the side of the working man. It was all very well knowing the Burletsons, Lord Joicey, Roddie Lambton — to name but a few of our capitalistic friends; the fact was, we'd experienced for ourselves the lot of the working class. No doubt, someone from an upper-class family who'd elected to live with a mining family in the Rhondda valley would have felt the same way. Times were very hard, whether one was a seaman or a miner.

The odd thing was almost no one grumbled or agitated. It was too soon after the great social revolution, brought about by the quite senseless waste of life in the Great War, caused in part by the rotten leadership of certain generals on the Western front but, to some extent, neutralised by the selfless courage shown by the officer class in the ordinary front-line regiments.

The favourite topic of conversation between my brother and I was the *Carslogie*. One of us invariably brought it up.

"How did you get on with Mr Robinson?" Bill asked about the second engineer.

"Very well; but there was a lot of trouble in Belfast. He went after Gwyn, the galley boy, with a carving knife."

"Drunk, was he?" asked Bill.

"Drunk as a lord."

"I suppose he thought Gwyn was after his wife? Funny how women on a ship always cause trouble," Bill remarked.

"Just imagine what it'd be like if they were allowed to come out to sea as well."

The *Carslogie* had been at Belfast for over a fortnight, being patched up after suffering heavy weather damage in the North Atlantic. The deck split in way of number three hold and the seawater leaked in and caused the grain cargo to swell. Because of the ship's enforced delay, several of the officers' wives came onboard for the duration of the visit. The smell of the contaminated grain as it was discharged manually in sacks was terrible and one had to hold one's nose to venture on deck.

"D'you remember the *Ullapool*?" asked Bill. "She too was a hard case, you know. I met someone who'd been donkey in her."

The donkeyman, the equivalent of the bosun, the most senior non~officer on deck, had certain privileges and usually stood the chief engineer's watch when at sea.

The conversation went on like this for hours. We'd indulge in reminiscence while walking up and down the East drive or in the smoking-room after dinner. We left my mother and her friends to gossip away in the green room while we sat in my father's study.

Sometimes we'd talk about the estate and the farms, but it was obvious even then that Bill wasn't very interested in country things. I think he liked the house though; we got along best there.

It was wonderful to come home and see the familiar scenes again. Lonely and isolated though it was, the wildness of sea and moor and hills engendered strange emotions. Despite the bitter cold and the tepid bath water, it was a lovely house to live in; light, graceful and airy with its Adam decoration; the beautiful shape of the oval rooms, the wide staircase of white stone with the glass dome above, through which we saw the moon, the shining stars or just the dark blue night sky as we went up to bed.

The room I liked best was the oval saloon, its doors topped by carved wooden pediments. Round the pale blue-green walls stood old embroidered chairs and dark paintings. The muted colours and the worn Persian carpets contrasted marvellously with the big vases of flowers which seemed to glow with brightness and life.

My mother spent hours arranging the vases in the spring with jonquils and lilies-of-the-valley. I preferred the autumn flowers: flaming azalea leaves, orange marigolds, enormous bunches of dahlias and montbretia, and found them in room after room.

Apart from our interest in ships and a few people whom we both knew, my brother and I grew to have little in common. In a way I feared him. Perhaps I still expected to be sent out of the room for behaving badly. I never disagreed with him or asked myself if I really liked him or not. We were linked by Barmoor, family and our love for our dead father. I took our relationship for granted, but it only went so far. We never once talked about girls or women; or that I spent so much time playing the Bechstein in the green drawing-room. An unspoken barrier existed between us; certain subjects were taboo. It wasn't until many years later that I stepped outside our tacitly agreed limits.

I survived the War thanks to the doctor attached to 138 Wing, Freddie Buckler. He'd been with 2 Group since the beginning of hostilities. When the 2nd Tactical Air Force came into being at the end of 1943, Doc was posted to the Mosquito Wing based at Lasham then. He went to the most remarkable lengths to look after the aircrews; nothing was too much trouble for him.

I didn't know it at the time, but after a daylight raid on Hamburg, when three Mosquito squadrons operating from Epinoy had a bad mauling, Doc went to the Commanding Officer, "Dopie" Bowers and insisted that Knight and I be taken off ops forthwith. Knight and I had more operational sorties than anyone. We were the only remaining survivors of 613 squadron. The third survivor, "Eggie" Gardner, had he been with us, would have been sent home as well, but he managed to force-land his badly damaged Mosquito in Sweden after the famous "daylight" on Hamburg. I never saw him again but was told that he'd come through the War well.

At the time of the raid on Hamburg, I didn't know that it was to be my last. It wasn't an easy trip and I'd been on the receiving end of a lot of flak; however I managed to return to base, unlike many of the others.

I couldn't believe it when I was told to pack my things and return to base. "Go home. You've had enough. Wait for a posting."

With three completed tours of ops certified in my log book, it was safe to assume that for me the fighting part of the war was over. Indeed I spent the next few months as an instructor, based first at Finmere and then at Middleton St George near Middlesbrough.

On the basis of first in, first out, I was soon demobilized and found myself back in "civvy" street. The first general election after the war gave Labour a landslide; Churchill was out. I couldn't believe the nation's verdict. I took it personally, Churchill had faults but he'd taken us to victory. How must he feel, I wondered; I too, felt aggrieved. I'd risked my life. I was a minor war hero, with a DFC and near 100 sorties; and yet all the things I'd fought for were being done away with; everything would be different from now on.

Under the terms of my father's will, I had been left a farm in Southern Rhodesia. There's no future in England, I thought; I'd best try my luck there!

My mind was made up but all attempts to get a passage in a ship going to Africa failed. I had a talk with my sister-in-law as soon as I could. Thanks to her efforts and Eric De La Rue's, her other brother-in-law, I found myself, within a matter of weeks, on the dockside at Birkenhead preparing to embark on the 5/5 *Clan Chisholm* loading for South Africa and Beira, the port of entry for Southern Rhodesia. Six years had passed since I'd been on board a cargo ship; but it seemed like only a few weeks, the smells and sounds were unchanged. I'm back, I thought.

The voyage to Cape Town took two weeks; I wish it'd taken two years, it was so wonderful to be on board ship again. After a few days, I was allowed to go anywhere I liked and got into a routine of watching the fires below for two hours each evening and spending the next two hours in the engine-room itself. Once we began the long leg down the coast of West Africa, I'd lie in the sun up on the fo'c'sle head and watch the flying fish leaping out of the sea just ahead of the ship's stem.

I'd time to reflect on my life. Was I too hasty leaving England? Should I have persevered in my effort to get into Lloyd's? Perhaps I should've approached someone else for advice? I didn't know anybody in the City, and when I asked my mother to help, she seemed surprised that I even asked if she knew any business men who might talk to me. "I can't think of anyone, darling," she said. "You see, darling, we're not a business family. We don't know any-one in the City."

To hear her talk one would have imagined that the City was some far-off island in the Pacific. Later I found out, she regularly went to lunch at the Great Eastern Hotel, Liverpool Street, with influential friends in that famous square mile. I can only imagine she wasn't focusing when I talked to her, for unknown reasons.

The days passed only too quickly on the *Clan Chisholm*. She was built during the war at Greenock to a pre-war design. A twin-screw ship, owned by Clan Line Steamers, she carried well over 10,000 tons of cargo. The crew thought the world of the owners, the Cayzer family. During the depression, the company didn't lay up a single ship, although cargoes were few and far between. No one got paid off. All the ships were kept at sea, somehow.

The best part of my day was going below after tea. The ship had six 60-ton boilers working on forced draught. The forward stoke-hold was very clean and peaceful compared to the other since the boilers used oil. Much to my delight, the other three burned coal. I persuaded the Lascar firemen to let me stand a watch with them. The engine-room was dominated by two large triple-expansion engines with exhaust turbines of the latest design with drop-valves on the high-pressure cylinders. I watched those reciprocating engines for hours.

I left the ship at Beira on the East coast of Africa and took the train to Salisbury, the capital of Southern Rhodesia, intending to visit the farm my father left me, but, even before I saw it, I realised that to make enough money to return to London and get into Lloyd's, I'd have to look farther afield. Though upset and depressed at England's lurch towards Socialism, I was determined to go back and live in the country I'd just fought for in war.

I spent the next two years in South Africa. During the early part, while staying in a very seedy hotel in Johannesburg, I made a bit of a living selling magazine advertising space. A European working in the city was expected to have a car, which was obtainable only on the black market; I couldn't afford it anyway. Worse than the endless tramping down hot streets was the loneliness. I dreaded Sundays with little to do; invariably, more out of desperation than anything else, I took a tram to the zoo, the only free entertainment there was.

Slowly, I met people and got a better job. An English couple had pity on me and allowed me to be a paying guest at their house in the suburbs. I took up flying again and spent much time at the Rand flying club where hiring an aeroplane wasn't expensive.

Then one of my mother's brothers died and left me £3,000. Six months later, after a gold strike in the Orange Free State, I turned it into £10,000 and thought seriously about going home to Lloyd's.

My mother wrote to me faithfully every week to tell me of events. With Bill married, she left Barmoor for a house in London. Some of her letters were very critical of her new daughter-in-law and hinted that the marriage wasn't a great success; I think my mother was secretly quite pleased.

By the time I returned to England, Bill and Betty had parted. My brother simply could not act the part of a country squire and Betty, at her age and with her upbringing, couldn't be expected to change either.

When the time came to decide about returning to England, I had doubts and misgivings. I'd landed a fine job and enjoyed my life in Port Elizabeth. Sally, a girl I was, to use the old-fashioned word, courting in England, made the difference. I tried to persuade her to join me in South Africa. I could imagine nothing better than to set up a home with her there. But, to my dismay, she wrote to say that she'd met a dashing young Army officer and was engaged to be married. Feeling rather sorry for myself, I came home.

Here we go again, I thought, as I sat in the long passage inside the main entrance to Lloyd's. I didn't try this time to see Mr Dick-Cleland; instead I managed to wangle an introduction to a Mr Lofthouse, who now approached me with outstretched hand.

My involvement with this new friend dragged on for week after week. "I'll be happy to take you on in my underwriting staff but I've a problem," he said. "I can't start you off till I have a larger box."

The box was actually a desk with seats in the Underwriting Room. It was here that I was to sit and work, but I sensed another problem; the business Mr Lofthouse underwrote had nothing whatsoever to do with ships.

After a month or two of waiting for news of when I could start, I gave up. What was the point, of being a clerk in a syndicate that apparently only insured the risks of common law liability?

Yet, after six months of frustration and disappointment, I did finally land as a clerk in the Life department of a large firm of Lloyd's insurance broker, Price Forbes and Company; I couldn't believe my luck. Better yet, after several months, the Company Secretary sent for me and asked if I was enjoying my job. I assured him that all was well, but that, if ever an opening in the firm's marine department came about, I'd like to be considered. Within a week, I was transferred.

I saw very little of Bill during those early years in the City, but every week my mother gave me news of him. First, the break-up of his marriage, then an expensive financial misadventure in the Channel Islands.

At Price Forbes I was so much older than the other "juniors", I had to work hard to establish myself. I'd the war to thank for that and the two years spent in South Africa. I was well enough liked by everyone but a long way behind. The only way to catch up, if I was determined, was to pass all the insurance exams. At least then I'd be better qualified technically, than the others.

It took three years to qualify. If it weren't for my long commute from Sussex to the City, and those two free hours each day sitting in a train, I wouldn't have succeeded, but I still didn't feel involved enough with my true love, the ship. After eight good years with Price Forbes, it was time to move on. An opportunity arose with H Clarkson and Company; an old established firm of shipbrokers who decided to invest and expand. At last I had what I wanted.

My wife, Phoebette, and my sister, Ann, loved to take all the children to Barmoor during the summer holidays. Anna still lived there but was married to Bill now. Betty, knowing about the baby, quickly divorced Bill and for a while, life was fairly normal.

Bill left his house every morning to catch the train to Newcastle where he'd a job, albeit unpaid. I didn't see a great deal of him; he seemed more withdrawn and moodier than ever and was prone to offer sarcastic comments about City business people like myself. "Where's your bowler?" he'd ask, and, "I thought you never went anywhere without your umbrella."

It was quite clear, he was envious or jealous or both. At times, we'd get back onto common ground: the pre-war tramp steamers we both loved; but our talks became rarer. It was thanks to my sister that everyone got on together, when the family went to Barmoor. She and Bill had always been close and fond of each other. Admittedly, their ages were more similar; they'd even overlapped at Oxford, and their bedrooms at Barmoor were at the other end of the house to mine. Bill's had been the night nursery originally. Both their rooms were down a little passage and caught the evening sun. The had a view of the pond garden and, separated by a ha-ha, a recessed wall below the line of sight, the fields beyond

My room was some away; much smaller and with a view over the big lawn in front of the house. From my window, the sea, only six miles off, looked very close at times, and occasionally I'd see a smudge of steam or smoke from a passing train, as the railroad followed the coast. At Cheswick it ran only a few hundred yards from the beach. No one liked my room very much; it caught the early morning sun only and for the rest of the day was rather gloomy. Worse was the fact, it adjoined the only haunted room in the house, the notorious "square room", which was absolutely square. Originally my bedroom was its dressing-room. Try as they might, no one, not even the estate carpenter, could make the connecting door stay shut. It terrified me. I slept with the light on in the passage outside, much to the irritation of Thomson, who always fussed about the drain on the storage batteries, which he had to keep charged.

The square room contained an enormous four-poster bed; a forbidding piece of furniture. It was an ordinary bedroom really but, unknown to visitors, another door hid behind a massive tallboy and gave access to a dark gloomy area, to this day unexplored. Rumour had it that somewhere in there was a bottomless shaft; Thomson had offered to go down into it on a rope but in the end he didn't; the square room was left with its secret.

On a visit to my mother's house in London, conveniently near Victoria station, where I caught my train to Horsham, she told me that Bill was very excited over the discovery of quality limestone on the estate. "Isn't it marvellous, darling? Bill will be rich at last."

The news genuinely pleased me. It was better than chopping away at the trees.

My mother went on: "He said in his letter that he was crushing the rock and selling it. He is clever, isn't he?"

"Lucky, you mean."

He says he bought an old steam-roller to drive the machine which crushes the rock."

I pricked up my ears. "Really?"

"And then he bought an old army lorry to take the limestone to the farms."

"That's marvellous," I said. So, the old boy had some enterprise after all. "Jolly good," I added. "I think that's terrific."

What a breakthrough, I thought. An opportunity arose for me to see for myself, and I asked Bill to put me up for some nights. "I'll only stay a few days; it's quite a time since we had a good crack." Meaning a "talk" in North Country.

I found my brother on the crest of a wave. "Hey!" he said quite excitedly after breakfast the first day. "Come to the smoking-room, look at all the orders I've got."

I knew he'd plenty of orders. I'd found some lying about on the floor of the bathroom.

"You don't understand," he harped. "You're used to the City. We do business differently up here. We don't need a bowler hat to get on, you know."

I remained silent, not reacting to his taunt.

I'd given up wearing a bowler hat when I joined Clarksons. Shipbrokers went about in soft hats and suede shoes.

"D'you know something?" he continued. "A hell of a lot of my business is done down in the Black Bull at Lowick, but I'll take you to the quarry. You'll get quite a surprise."

We walked across the fields toward Barmoor Mill Farm. The quarry had.been transformed, an enormous shed erected, with conveyor belts snaking here and there and a line of lorries waiting to be loaded under a large hopper.

"There now; what d'you think of that, Mister?" It'd been years since Bill had addressed me in such an intimate way. "Mister" was reserved for special occasions. "What d'you think of that, eh?"

"Fantastic," I murmured, Christ, how bloody marvellous. I was genuinely impressed; to think he'd started out with an old steam-roller and a hired crusher! "Fantastic," I repeated. "But where are all the men? Having a break?"

Nothing moved. There was no noise, or sign of life.

My brother beckoned me; I followed him obediently. "Come this way," he said. " We'll go and see why they've knocked off."

Surely they can't be having a strike, I thought. I was used to that in the shipyards, but not here. I followed Bill into a Nissen hut at the side of the quarry, full of men playing cards; one stood as Bill entered. "I was just coming to the Castle to see you, Mr Bill."

"What's the matter?" asked my brother.

"It's yon belt, Mr Bill." The man spoke with a strong Northumbrian accent. "It's split and won't stay on the pulley."

Bill stood there saying nothing.

"Shall I send wee Alec away to get another?" the man asked.

"Areet," said my brother, using the local pronunciation.

I squirmed. We left the hut without a next word. I could sense Bill's mood take a turn for the worse.

I tried to sound cheerful. "I don't suppose it'll take them long to get a new one. We can come again in the morning to see the plant working; I'm not going off until the evening."

"It'll take them longer than that," he replied gloomily. "They'll have to send a lorry to Leeds."

"To Leeds!" I exclaimed. "Why Leeds? That's 200 miles away!"

"I know, I know. There's no need to go on about it."

I said nothing more, but almost shook my head in disbelief. We trudged back to the house silently. When Bill suggested a drink that evening in the Black Bull, I readily agreed.

In the village pub we enjoyed a game of dominoes.

"Can I have a word with you, Mr Bill?" I recognised the speaker as having been around since before the war.

Bill nodded and asked the man what he'd like to drink.

"It's like this, Mr Bill." The man paused to light a cigarette. "I'll be finishing on the roads in another couple of weeks; d'you think there'd be a job for me down at the quarry?"

I looked at my brother. "Yes," he answered with a frown. "I'm sure we can find you one; come see me when you're ready."

The man touched his cap and got up. "That's very good of you, Mr Bill; very good of you."

Bill smiled and nodded.

"That's areet, Bapty," he said.

I returned to London, worried; Bill had a full order book, but clearly he'd no idea of how to run a business. Why didn't he keep spare parts on hand? He'd shown me a long list of farms using his lime, and another book giving the total earned, month by month. The cash flow did look impressive enough, but the basics of tax provisions, depreciation, and elementary amortization were completely absent from Bill's mind.

During the next two years, my anxieties about Bill and Barmoor grew. Yet, all seemed well, for the time being. I relied on the weekly visits to my mother for news.

With President Nasser closing the Suez canal, I had problems of my own. A major oil company and Clarkson client, needed an insurance scheme to take into account the uncertainty ahead. I had to work out the complications.

One day quite by chance, I bumped into a man who owned farms near Alnwick, thirty miles south of Barmoor. "It's a pity about your brother selling Brackenside," he said quite casually.

Brackenside was the best farm on the estate. I was horrified.

I told my mother. "Bill sold Brackenside to one of the Barbers."

"I don't believe it," she answered.

"Honestly, Mama. Why should Willie Renwick made that up?"

"Sold Brackenside? What rubbish! Bill's coming South next week," she added. "I expect you'll be seeing him, won't you?"

I sighed. Since my grandfather died, not an acre of the estate had been sold, after six or so were put up to meet death duties.

MY BROTHER and I met in the City. I could sense, he regarded that part of London with the deepest suspicion.

"Let's go to the Jamaica and have a sherry," I said.

We talked away about this and that, all the usual topics. I was embarrassed to bring up Brackenside; he'd probably tell me to mind my own business and be quite within his rights. And yet, Barmoor and the estate was a family matter. It'd been the Sitwell home for hundreds of years and should remain so. My brother may've inherited everything there; nobody objected to that, but by so doing he was, in effect, custodian. It should be handed down as intact as possible to the next generation.

"Well, I must be getting along, " he said, finishing his drink.

The time was now or never. "Is it true you've sold Brackenside?"

I asked trying to sound casual and vague, as if wanting to know whether the Number 11 bus went to Hammersmith.

No," he replied, after a pause, "I haven't." He made to leave.

"Any other questions?" he added sarcastically.

I felt my courage evaporating, I still feared him in an odd way. "No," I murmured.

We shook hands.

"Give my love to Phoebette," he said.

Turning on his heel, he walked away.

Back at the office I stared at the papers on my desk wondering.

Another year went by. I didn't mention the farm again to my mother; it'd only put her in a bad temper. My sister, however, came to stay with me in Sussex for a few days and made a chance remark which increased my anxiety about the estate.

"Have you lent Bill any money?" she asked suddenly.

I was taken aback. How on earth could he have asked Ann for money? She was perpetually hard up. I would've thought it'd be the other way round. "No," I answered. "Why?"

She realised she'd been indiscreet and coloured slightly.

"Oh, nothing really," she murmured.

"Has he asked you for some then?"

"Well, I think he's finding it hard to pay the rates."

"The rates?"

"Yes. Surely you knew he was terribly broke."

"I suspected things weren't going too well, but not that bad."

"I'm afraid it is."

"I was told he'd sold Brackenside."

I thought she was going to cry. "Poor old Bill," she said. "I wish I could help him. I'd ask James but I know my husband needs every penny for his architectal business just now."

"Bill must be pretty desperate if he's asked you for money," I said. Any minute now and he'll sell another farm, I thought. Perhaps he already has! He was obviously worse off than I realised. No wonder I'd been kept in the dark. He'd do anything to hold the truth from me; I could just imagine what he'd said to Ann: "Ask Simon to help me! Not bloody likely, the lousy little know-all!"

I was at the bottom of the garden one summer's evening when a yell came from the house. "Telephone!"

"Who is it?" I asked.

"I think it's Thomson," said my wife.

My heart sank. It had to be bad news. He'd never phoned me before. "Hullo."

"Is that you, Master Simon?"

"Yes. What's up?"

"D'ye know where Mr Bill is?"

"No, I don't."

"He's gone, Master Simon. No one knows where he is; not even Mr Bolam."

"What's happening, Thomson?" I asked, dreading the reply.

"The Castle's up for sale and the drives full of cars and people wanting to see over the house."

I gasped. "Send them away, Thomson. I'll come up tomorrow."

I put down the receiver, my head spinning. The inevitable had happened.

It didn't make sense. My father was a Brigadier General, who never quit even in the most trying of times, but Bill had fled much like a scared rabbit from his own hounds, that he'd set on himself.

Ann marrying her first husband

ANN

I'M SURE my love of history came from my father. He was a soldier first but, when he had the time, after retiring from the Army, he wrote two outstanding books, considered authoritative works on their particular subjects: the keeps and castles of the Border and archaeological finds in the North of England.

I'm sure my mother loved him very much but, for all that, he appeared isolated from her and her friends. I picture him now at his desk in the smoking-room, as we children called it, but really his study, writing for hours on end while puffing at a cigarette. Bill told me that he smoked one hundred a day; Capstan, full strength, they came in an oblong yellow box.

I was nineteen and up at Oxford when the doctors found he had cancer. Those last few months before he died, the summer of 1932, were horrible; he hurt so much. The only drug we had was morphine then; everyone knew what happened if you took too much; that's why he endured the pain so bravely.

Now that I'm grown up, I look at Bill and Simon and try to find my father's traits in them. I see how they react to different things and try to imagine how Deedle would've behaved.

He had a very tough upbringing; first Harrow, then Sandhurst, where cadets get up at some unearthly hour for a five-mile run, before plunging into a cold bath to be ready for the early morning parade. It must've been dreadful but I daresay they accept it as part of the course; after all, it's a considerable achievement to pass into the Royal Military College.

Life was not the same after he died; I felt protected by him. He was so proud of me. He did his best to see that I was nicely dressed and a credit to the family. I'm sure my mother did care about me but it wasn't very apparent. She seemed quite out of touch with people my age, and gradually I found myself living in the past; Mary, Queen of Scots; Oliver Cromwell; Charles the First. They fascinated me; the history of England is such a rich pasture; I'd dream for hours, graze on those lush acres of intrigue. When the time came to leave West Heath, my school, I had the very good fortune to get a scholarship to Somerville College, Oxford.

I'd little in common with my brothers; we were so unalike. In the War years, after I first married, I got to know Bill much better and we enjoyed meeting and telling each other stories. With Simon it was different; he was always so serious and nearly always proved to be right. It was quite uncanny, how in the end his predictions came true. My mother used to scoff at him, but she knew very well that he was talking sense; however my mother, for all her many virtues, didn't enjoy facing facts. Because of this I suspect, Simon reacted by taking life a little too seriously. I knew that irritated Bill and even I found it a little tedious; Simon had a good sense of humour, but if he felt strongly about something, he'd pursue it to the bitter end. Bill, on the other hand, was too like my mother; he hated facing the truth and went to great lengths to avoid anything controversial.

I married Cub Hartley in 1937; having met him at Oxford. Everything went swimmingly for a few years but, after the War started, he joined the Air Force, and I'm afraid I became bored with him, and we parted. Looking back, I think he was supremely patient with me. I was influenced at Oxford by the "New Left" and felt it to be my duty to go to the aid of the oppressed working classes in Spain when their civil war was in progress.

But, alas, I never went. Some great friends of mine, Anastasia and Igor Anrep, white Russians, persuaded me to go to Vienna instead to help bring to England Jewish refugees from Hitler's persecutions. I absented myself in the process from my husband, who by then was a master at Eton, and became very involved in politics as well. I'd disappear to Cornwall or places equally remote to make speeches for Labour Party candidates in by-elections. No wonder my poor husband got fed up.

I didn't see a great deal of my family while this was going on. Bill gave me away at my wedding, a smart occasion at the Temple in London; Simon was an usher; they both liked my husband very much. I liked him too, for that matter, but I was far too flighty, a characteristic I am sure I inherited from my mother.

When I divorced, my mother made light of it and even thought it amusing; she made no attempt to scold me or point out how stupidly I'd behaved. In her lack of concern, her children could do no wrong; later on, unfortunately she behaved similarly over Bill. Simon, her favourite, automatically was forgiven for anything and everything. After eleven years of marriage, he abandoned his wife and two young children. He was full of remorse and admitted he'd no justification for behaving so heartlessly; not so my mother. She argued that what he'd done was justified and understandable.

In future years, when problems surrounding Bill and Barmoor fell on Simon's shoulders, Simon complained to me: our mother did little or nothing to stop Bill from behaving as he did.

"If only she'd put her foot down, Bill would've had second thoughts," Simon often said.

But I rarely agreed with him; after all, who was I to moralise!

During the War, I worked at the Ministry of Information. It suited me better than one of the Services, who wouldn't have kept me for long. I'm absolutely hopeless when it comes to cars or anything mechanical. I was also terribly vague. I lose much and often miss trains much to the despair of my family. Teaching history was what I liked doing best and after a few years at the MOI, as the Ministry of Information was called, I went and taught at a girls' school on the South coast.

I also tried to write a book about the family, but didn't get very far. I daresay, if I'd tried a bit harder and spent weeks at Barmoor going through old letters and such, I might've succeeded. I'm still fascinated by Frank Sitwell, the younger brother of Sitwell Sitwell, who inherited Renishaw. The things Frank did at Barmoor were quite bizarre; follies all over the place; some of the buildings at the farm nearest the house were adorned with battlements to conform to the skyline of the Castle which lay out of sight. Also, the enormous farm buildings were built so as to accommodate visitors to an agricultural show, which he insisted be held at Barmoor. One huge building, used to house cattle in the winter-time, began as a banqueting hall; tents would've sufficed but my extravagant forefather always went with excess.

He must've lost most of his money, as he had to flee to France to escape his creditors; there's even one story that he faked his death and then went, disguised, to his own funeral.

A great horseman, very proud of his hounds, he once wagered twelve gold goblets that his pack would kill more fox before sundown than a neighbour's. Large tracts of land were wagered away equally stupidly. I've heard that we Sitwells owned an enormous amount of land stretching right across Glendale to the Cheviots. A hill called Yeavering Bell, near Wooler, certainly belonged to the family. Simon wanted his fighter aircraft named after it, but decided on *Grey County* instead, for the wet skies of Northumberland. I thought it rather sensible of the Air Force to let a fighter pilot keep his own aeroplane; a bit like having one's own horse. Simon said he spent hours polishing his plane.

I loved listening to my father tell me about Northumberland; I often went with him on his expeditions. He told me: large tracts of the country hadn't altered since the Roman occupation; the population, once extensive, has nearly disappeared. Sheep have replaced the wild animals, and fences demarcate the hill farms, but it's not difficult to realise that we're seeing the long ago, as the inhabitants of those days left their mark on the banks of many a lonely burn. Three places fascinated my father absolutely; all showed traces of an ancient cult and were almost in sight of each other. Yeavering Bell with its beautiful conical shape was one of them; a triple circle of stones engirdled its summit. And it had an unmistakable causeway from the apex exactly oriented to midwinter sunrise. An even more extraordinary alignment was at Duddo, nine miles north from Yeavering. Whichever way any two of the five standing stones were aligned, one got either a cardinal point of the compass or the direction of a midsummer, midwinter, or equinoctial sunrise. My father's theory was that these marked an ancient burial site.

Routing Lynn was the third place. We went often for its beauty. Here, a stream that drained Barmoor South Moor and Ford Moss attained the dignity of a waterfall, some 20 feet in height. By the side of the small and lonely road, connecting the main Berwick-to-Wooler turnpike with the Till Valley by way of Kimmerston at

Red Scar Bridge, lies a stone hidden in heather and bracken. As the crow flies, this rock is exactly five miles north-east of Yeavering Bell, which is in full view. Concentric circles around a center hole cover this rock, from which leads a duct. My father believed the carvings were the handiwork of the Picts since traces of Pictish dwellings exist on the adjacent hill above Fenton, where his friend, Lord Durham, lived. Similar marks could be found on the top of Berwick Law, eleven miles away to the south-east; these marks probably were religious.

Berwick Law, on the Chatton to Alnwick road, was among my favourite places; a steep bluff and one of the tallest hills in the Kyloe range, its situation was glorious. Looking westward across the valley, Hedgehope and Cheviot dominated the landscape; to the south-west one looked up the valley of the Breamish, six miles to Ingram. On the east, the purple moors stretched away as far as the eye could see, with a glimpse of the sea beyond. Only one habitation was visible and it bore the suggestive name of Blaw Weary; Simonside and Rothbury forest formed the horizon to the south. I loved Northumberland; the names have such a romantic sound to them; and the history is so strong.

I never understood why my mother didn't spend more time at Barmoor. She was an accomplished artist, with a good eye for colour; I thought she should've liked nothing better than going with my father, taking her sketch book with her, and painting while he prodded away at his beloved rocks and ancient stones.

I understood that she preferred London, as she found the endless gossip about hounds and record grouse bags boring. I was far too frightened of my Northumbrian contemporaries to form a real opinion; I was always so conscious of my wretched clothes and my shyness. To be asked to play tennis caused me sleepless nights; I agreed to go, though I'd never had a tennis lesson in my life and didn't even know how to score. I was equipped with a broken old racket which my sweet cousin, Jean Gladstone, had given me. Everyone kept telling me how pretty I was, which was little comfort when I knew I looked shabbier than the village girls. When I first went to Oxford, it took me quite a long time to get used to being thought attractive, as that often came first.

I never lived in Northumberland again after I got married, though whenever I'd the chance, I went back to revisit those lovely places I knew as a girl.

With the war ended, I remarried and settled in London. All my friends seemed to be there, and thanks to people like Elizabeth Jenkins and Rosamund Lehman, I lived a very complete life, my desire for good conversation being satiated and nourished.

It was nice to have my mother in London as well. We met regularly to discuss speeches made at Chatham House or talk about some book one of us had read. Hardly a week passed without my going to the London library; I read endlessly.

My new husband, James Cubitt, bought a house not far from Baker Street, in York Terrace, on the edge of Regent's park; it was ideal for taking our young son out in his pram. The Doric House, as it was called, was a superb example of Georgian architecture.

I never got tired of sitting in those beautifully proportioned rooms with their great big windows. During that period of my life I felt curiously relaxed and happy. Bill and Simon seemed to be quite settled, certainly Simon had a good job in the City and a very sweet wife. She and I took our families to Barmoor each summer.

The children obviously adored the place and, as they got older, I told them the history of the Castle. It was originally nothing more than an oblong hold for forty horsemen, Halfway between Berwick and Wooler, it made an admirable rallying place to aid the nearby castles lying in the valley of the river Till, a tributary of the Tweed. Barmoor was spelt Beyimoor then, and Byermore, signifying the Bare Moor, part of the Barony of Wooler, a small market town at the foot of the Cheviots.

Watchlaw and Woodside, both on the Barmoor estate, formed part of an elaborate system of look~outs, as they commanded immense views into Scotland. Under the ever-present threat of a raid from the Highlands, Duddo tower kept watch on the lower Till valley and parts of the Tweed as far as Norham, with its proud Castle built in 1121. At the first sign of a raid, a flare at Woodside warned Haggerston and Kyloe, whence the alarm went direct to

Bamburgh Castle, perhaps the oldest in England. From there, the news spread down our wild and craggy coast. Watchlaw roused Wooler and Hepburn Bell and old Bewick, which passed the news to the valleys of the Breamish. Each Castle paid a price. It's said, Berwick had more sieges than any town in history save Jerusalem.

Muschamp of Barmoor crenellated the square hold in 1341. By adding battlements, he made Barmoor permanent. In the fifteenth century, Barmoor still belonged to the Muschamp family, but they were ruined by the Civil War and the fines exacted by Parliament, so the Castle went by marriage to the Carr family, from nearby Etal. A gentleman, Samuel Phipps acquired it in 1723 and left it, in 1791, to his cousin Francis Sitwell of Renishaw, whose elder brother Sitwell Sitwell was created a baronet in 1808.

Being so interested in history, I found Bamburgh Castle the more exciting. It's recorded in the Romance of Arthur as "Joyous Guarde" but its name derives from Queen Bebba, the wife of Ethelfrid, King of Northumbria. He gave her the town and called the place Bebbanburg after her. The great fortress was set on fire in A.D. 685 by Penda, King of Mercia, but after his defeat and death, Bamburgh remained the capital of Northumbrian kings for nearly 100 years. From A.D. 925 onwards, Danes and Norsemen struggled for its possession. By the time William the First had completed his conquest in A.D. 1069, Bamburgh, York, and Durham were the only inhabited towns left in the North. And, in 1348, a great plague also devastated the Border.

During the fifteenth century, Bramburgh changed hands continually. In 1462 it was held by the Yorkists but within a year it fell to the French for the second time. Like its neighbour, Dunstanburgh Castle, farther down the coast, it was stormed by Henry VI supporters and became a ruin; uninhabitable, it played no further part in official history.

A survey of the Border strongholds in 1542 describes Bamburgh as still ruinous after its bombardment nearly 100 years before. Even Barmoor is stated as in "extreme decay and almost ruynous for lack of reparacions". Norham was in decay too. Only Haggerston had a strong tower in good repair, lived in by the Leylands.

Lord Crewe, last of the Prince Bishops of Durham, bought Bamburgh in 1704 from the Fosters, who had "squandered their patrimony". Not only did Lord Crew restore it but, on his death in 1722, founded the Crewe Trust. In 1893, Lord Armstrong purchased Bamburgh, and because of my mother's friendship with his wife, I often stayed there.

The Dane's Graveyard, a bare and sinister place, among the sand dunes, lies a quarter mile from the Castle. A famous London surgeon and historian opened the ground in the 1920s and came on a double circle of stones; two feet below the surface he found the skeleton of a man showing the wound that killed him. The position of the limbs proved that he'd stiffened before burial and never been straightened; blood marks were visible near the thorax after more than 800 years. My father believed that the corpse had been hastily thrust into a half-filled grave containing heathen Danes, and not allowed in consecrated ground within the castle wall.

At the moment of discovery, a terrific squall blew over Bamburgh. The diggers intended to explore further but a deputation from the village forbade them. Any small disturbance of the Dane's Graveyard invariably brought bad weather; the squall did cause several fishing boats to cut free their nets and run for shelter.

Thanks to my father, I learnt a great deal too about his mother's ancestors, the d'Oliers. Names amused me, as they changed so much over time. Whether Dilston Castle was built by D'Eivill, tempo Henry I, or Dyvelstones, tempo Henry II, is one example, but definitely the Devil's Water nearby takes its name from this unconstant family.

All I have now are my father's books. I was different from Bill and Simon and grown up when Dad became ill. I think he knew this, that I'd inherited from him a deep love for the past. He so delighted in talking to me. I used to sit with him for hours on end.

My mother apparently disliked his mother very much. She had lived in the Dower house at Barmoor, at the end of the garden. I don't remember her as she died when I was only a child, but I recall my mother describing her as a rather disagreeable woman who was so Irish that she could hardly speak English.

After Deedle died, I tried to find out more about the Irish branch of my family but my mother always changed the subject; she was quite determined not to discuss matters which bored her. I never knew, for example, that my father had, as a young man, first married a very beautiful English girl called Constance Meade who died of peritonitis or some inoperable ailment. A plaque on the wall of Lowick church attests to her memory and says that she was buried at Bradford-on-Avon. My father never talked about her; nor did anybody else.

The d'Oliers were a very distinguished family. My father's research only went back as far as 1656 when Edouard Olier became the Marquis of Nointel, although a Betrand Olier was Capitoul of Toulouse. They all lived in the South of France and held high offices under the French kings, inter-marrying with the Colberts, Malherbes, Beauregards and other illustrious lines. Edouard had three sons. The youngest, Pierre, father of Isaac Olier, fled from France at the time of the Revocation and entered the service of William, Prince of Orange; in 1686 he was made a burger of the City of Amsterdam. However, he settled in Dublin and, having become a freeman of that city, changed his name to d'Olier in 1697. His grandson, Jeremiah, was high sheriff in 1788 and one of the principal streets in the city, d'Olier Street, is named after him. This remarkable man was a founder of the Bank of Ireland; he was its governor as was his relative, Isaac d'Olier. Isaac was the father of Ogle d'Olier, whose daughter "Cushy" was my father's mother.

I always wondered why Bill and Simon appeared so totally uninterested in things like this. To me, the d'Oliers were fascinating, far more than the Talbots, my mother's family. The d'Oliers had extra drive and ability, to re-establish themselves twice in different countries, first Holland and then in Ireland. Portraits of Jeremiah and Isaac d'Olier hang in the boardroom of the Bank of Ireland to this day, I'm told.

The history of Barmoor didn't interest my brothers either but they were very fond of the place and knew its industrial history; the coal mines and the limestone works.

Bill had gone to Oxford, read Geography, and was actually quite

well-informed about the geology of the country around Barmoor.
Simon was fascinated by the farms' ancient threshing machines;
they were miniature factories with permanently-installed boilers
and steam-engines. Simon once pointed out to me the complicated
shafts and pulleys and gear wheels made of wood. He had a map
on the wall of his bedroom, with little coloured flags showing
which farms still had machinery intact; only two of the original
engines remained; he wanted the Science Museum in London to
have one.

I never got to the bottom of Bill's business affairs in those years
after the War. Being married to Anna and travelling to work in
Newcastle every day produced his most stable period. Still, Simon
told me Bill worked for nothing then and how silly he was to be
doing so; I daresay Simon was right.

I've always been quite hopeless over money and business; my
poor husband, James, must have despaired of me at times. Nevertheless, we were very happy together; I think perhaps he found my
ignorance of financial matters quite amusing.

We had to cope with Anna and her son when her marriage to
Bill broke up. He wasn't very regular at paying her an allowance. I
felt sorry for her; James and I did our best to help and found her a
place to live in Eastbourne. After Bill vanished, Anna had nothing.
My mother and Simon between them made arrangements. Simon
also made a covenant to pay for the boy's education.

When Simon gave me the news that he was on his way North,
having heard from Thomson that Bill was missing and Barmoor
up for sale, my worst fears were confirmed. I'd given Bill money
from time to time, but couldn't really take it in, when Simon told
me what might happen. I prayed he'd save the situation. Yet, my
own father, the General, in his book about Northumberland had
talked about one family after another who routinely lost a farm or
two, even a Castle as well, due to profligacy, and Bill knew that too.

✳ Conty ✳

I've always kept diaries, since the age of thirteen, as the living of life seemed extraordinarily important and precious to me. I don't understand why, except for the stubborn inborn belief, growing stronger with the years, that nothing is really lost, that somehow, somewhere, days and years will be repeated, judged and enriched.

My home, when I was a girl, was Marchmont, a Georgian house near Hemel Hempstead, in Hertfordshire. It stood, not large, on a rise looking over a green valley with a flowing stream; on the other side of the house ran the road carrying its own trickle of breath.

High elders stood in the grass fields sloping down to the river; thorn trees and curly alders grew by its banks. The house always seemed full of life in those days; its atmosphere light-hearted, fresh and innocent. Most conversations were held in rooms with doors half open, or on the tall stairs. Sounds of whistling, singing, or the piano being played were continually in the air. Lots of friends and neighbours came in and out, and bevies of relatives. I had a shore-less sea of cousins, my grandfather having been one of the eight sons of the Lord Shrewsbury of an earlier generation.

For me the schoolroom, upstairs, was the centre of the house, with its view of the valley. Gustavus Talbot was my father's name, and Susan Elwes my mother's. She came from Norfolk and she, too, belonged to a large family who provided us with many first cousins, Birkbecks, Elweses, Dawnays, all living in Norfolk.

Those days are still so present to me, I can easily imagine myself sitting by the schoolroom window on a summer's afternoon, looking out; it is Sunday, perhaps, and my father and mother are playing croquet; I can hear the crack of the balls being hit. The cow-parsley is growing tall under the chestnut trees on the way to the river, and someone in grey flannels is fishing upstream. Yes, I see some visitors walking across the lawn. Who are they? My heart beats quicker. This dress, is it clean enough or muddy round the hem from walks in the garden? Long dresses with frills are the fashion after all. How many will there be for tea, I wonder? Will they come in here? The room smells so sweet with syringa in vases.

I'D NEVER SEEN Barmoor, my husband's home in the North, until 1913 by which time I'd been married a year. Nor had I ever been to Northumberland, except for passing through to Edinburgh. It'd always been exciting, to look out the train window for the first glimpse of the sea, to make out the low outline of Holy Island in the haze with the castle standing up at one end. Then came the short-bitten turf on the cliff near Berwick with the sea breaking below; this led on to the great moment of the train crossing the slow-flowing Tweed by the Border Bridge.

I remember getting out of the train for the first time when it pulled up at Berwick and breathing the invigorating, if chill, air that blows there. The chauffeur drove me to Barmoor back across the Tweed by a lovely old stone bridge, weathered a silver-pink, which after all these years of familiarity, still delights my eyes. From the road, after a few miles, I can see, faint in the distance, the pile of Bamburgh and the long line of the Cheviot Hills.

I don't think the truest of its lovers can claim gaiety or lightness of heart for the Northumbrian scene. It's a hybrid country, only half-English, a wedge that juts up into Scotland, with so many Scottish characteristics. I find it challenging and spacious, but rather bare. For all its noble outlines and the sense of history, it's never really taken me captive, though it fascinates my husband. But it offers some things the South of England can not give. Once, on a beautiful day, bright and windy, Willie and I set off on a long walk to climb the Cheviot. On a trail running between the green shoulders of hills, I couldn't resist going down to the burn that ran through the valley to see what shone so brightly yellow along its banks. Coming nearer, I found it to be mimulus in bloom; golden, blotched with brown and maroon and seeming to rejoice in the sun and sparkling water.

Beyond Langleyford was lovely; very tall firs grew there. The tang of resin in the air and the freshness of the scents gave the place an almost foreign air. We climbed over stone walls covered with foxgloves, their lilac-pink so tender in all the green. Then we followed a path mounting upward through birch and alder trees which showed us a stream hurrying and splashing down, leaving behind dark pools where the peaty water, pure and brown and dashed with foam, swirled and churned round the rocks. Honeysuckle hung over the dripping sides and ferns grew in the clefts, forever trembling and sprinkled with drops. From the soft and mossy path we emerged onto the windswept brightness of the hillside where rushing air drummed in our ears and whirled about us.

Climbing to the top was exhausting; we rested from time to time, lying down in the heather and bilberries, the wind racing over us and the brilliant sky above. The top, when we reached it, was a savage-looking spot of harsh grass and bog. We jumped from hassock to hassock to reach the cairn which marked the summit.

What a joy it was to turn downward again, wild with hunger, mind and limb dancing with life. The vast view of pale green slopes, pale blue distance and the far faint sea spread out below was something I shall never forget.

Living in a house within sight of the sea and able to look at it every day was new to me. I never became quite accustomed to the wonder of it, on a fresh autumnal morning, to see the sea, celadon-green and translucent, motionless, just before the light comes, or to catch the sun itself rising and slowly pouring its golden flood over the water and the land.

On fine days we went to Cheswick. Farther along, beyond the salmon nets, rose Bamburgh Castle, massive, royal-looking and unmistakable. Beyond the rocks lay Berwick, faint-coloured and lilac-grey.

Now it's Sunday afternoon; the light is dwindling but there's a nice fire. I hear the children playing upstairs but I'm alone in the green drawing-room, this oval space with its Chinese paper, green and flowery, and the lilac primulas in pots.

This morning, I wrote a long letter to Edith Sitwell. It's strange to think that we are related now. I knew her long before I met Willie, when I was a young woman and used to stay at Renishaw and Scarborough. Renishaw was a lovely house; it seemed Italian with its dark-blue tapestries, inlaid cabinets and stamped velvet and gold chairs, great vases of roses, and a Perugino picture. There seemed only a thin veil between the supernatural and the place, as in *John Inglesant*, the romance, as if ghosts walked about the house, though they liked the quiet of the great drawing-room with its musty smell best.

"Yes, it's as if someone dead is always there," Edith said.

I loved her mother, Lady Ida, from the first. Tall and handsome with a slightly lisping voice; she wore tweeds and a handkerchief knotted round her neck and a veil over her hat out-of-doors. Sir George seemed almost seventeenth-century with his punctilious little bows and stiff speeches; but I liked him too.

Osbert was there, and Sachie too, and a gentleman-tutor they called Gibbs, who was by way of making the boys sporting and getting them out-of-doors. He was very tall, with a mysteriously sad face; Lady Ida named him "the mystery" and her one aim in life seemed to be to get his "secret" out of him. Edith had an idea that he'd been cashiered from the Army and had led a "wild life" in America.

Even as the garden flowers blazed in the colours of paradise, I saw beyond the pale smoke of the tall chimneys from the iron-works. At night this was quite awesome. The inferno behind the park, its furnaces always going, lit the sky with a red glow.

I sketched the garden from the ballroom window while Edith played the Intermezzos of Brahms. Later in the garden, I sketched the long green avenue beyond the wooden gates as we sat by the Verona marble fountains. Then we drove to Chesterfield to visit a rose garden, rather a dreary proceeding; Lady Ida wasn't in good spirits and Edith never uttered a word. I talked to Sachie most of the time about Mars and the stars; his voice is a delight.

The next morning I went for a long expedition with Sachie on the roof. We tried to persuade Henry, the butler, and John, the footman, to come with us, but they had to wait on Sir George. I like him so much. It pleased me in a way to see him, with his pe-culiar good looks and his pompous manners, with portraits of his sixteenth-century ancestors around him.

On Christmas holiday in 1908, I stay with the family at Scar-borough where they often spent the winter. Osbert and Sachie were waiting in the marble pillared hall, with its two large vases of laurels. We proceeded to the billiard room for tea. Osbert is such an aristocrat and looks like one too, with his indolent, fair, rather cross face and tall, powerful form. And Sachie, with his deep voice and his mannered way of doing all the tiniest things. I really am fond of them; they're so familiar and friendly. I was surprised at how glad I was to be there. Later, Lady Ida came in from playing bridge, with a huge bunch of gardenias tucked into her black dress.

Henry, the butler from Renishaw, was there, as charming and loquacious as ever; always coming to the door with something unnecessary to say!

The house was an odd mixture of extreme comforts; the all-pervading smell of gardenias, white lilac and carnations; the big vase of tuberoses, the soft sofas and wood fires, good coffee and cigarettes; the feeling that no one need do anything, and the more money they spent, the better. The pianola played and there were meals of caviare and grapes and quails.

The last evening I was there, Edith, the boys, and I went for a long walk. The lighthouse was working, throwing its long shaft over the moving, troubled sea to one side, and to the other, over the harbour, calm and full of ships which had come home again to safety. We went to the sea wall and looked over. The high water was deep and dark, gurgling, sucking, curling and surging, so deep that it seemed, if all the world of men were dropped in it, it would cover them all and not be disturbed or wake the grim castle cliff or disturb the outline of the shore.

HERE I AM AGAIN in my beloved green drawing-room at Barmoor, the blank pages of my diary looking up at me almost accusingly.

What have I done this week? The hounds met in front of the house one morn. Willie was terribly pleased and made sure every-one had a glass of cherry brandy. He'd spent hours pressing the drink, from the black Morello cherries that grow on the kitchen garden wall. The colours of the morning are so cheerful; red coats, white hounds, green lawn and blue sea. I followed on foot with Ann and Bill for two hours; we saw a hunted fox slink along under a hedge. It's odd how exciting it is when hounds suddenly give tongue and come streaming through; nothing in the world seems so thrilling.

I'm back in the green drawing-room again with a warm fire. I've taken off my muddy brown tweed and put on a warm blue dress and sash, all suitable for a cosy evening. The house is very quiet; Willie hasn't come in yet; the servants live in a nether world here, as all the living rooms are on the first floor.

With the children here from school, the average day is a rather rough-and-tumble, nursery-ish affair. They all rush up and down stairs, with their endless talk of model railways. Bill and Simon are making a water-wheel in one of the wet ditches near the house.

A hot day in Northumberland is unusual; it makes the place seem different and almost strange; there's only the breath of a breeze from the hills now with barely a hint of vigour in it.

Earlier Willie and I walked through one of the woods, slowly, for Willie slashed at any thistle or nettle he saw. A silvery light fell on everything; the ferns, the trunks of the oaks and the Scotch firs. The ground was still damp from the heavy rains and my feet constantly sank in the peaty mould, leaving an imprint which quickly filled with brown water.

"I want to see if the orchises are out in the boggy field," I said.

"I'd rather come across some young partridge," he answered, disappointed with the game as he'd seen. "All drowned in the last rains," he muttered gloomily.

We walked on and came out on the other side of the wood. Willie went on to look at a young plantation, leaving me alone. Here and there, I came across an orchis, some purple, some red, and a few quite pale and frail with spotted, pointed leaves. Farther on, I came across the heart of their kingdom ringed around with bog-myrtle, but in the middle, secret, unseen, unknown, were growing the orchises of royal colour. Large, juicy-stalked and erect, they lifted themselves clear of the wet grass and water-mint, proud in their Tyrian purple.

I'LL ALWAYS REMEMBER the first thrill of seeing Bamburgh, standing against the sea; the long lines of the Castle along the great pile of rock, against an evenly white sky. It made a rather austere picture on a sunless day.

The Keep stands square above all the rest, exposed to the four winds; looking out mile beyond mile over the sand-dunes, coast line and the far hills. On the night I arrived to stay, I leant out the high window of my room, wanting to see the Farne Islands again. The beam from the lighthouse on the Inner Farne swept round, and I thought of poor Grace Darling rowing through those heavy seas to rescue the survivors from the Forfarshire.

The next morning broke on a leaden Northern day and every-one shivered in the chill air in the open boat on the way to the farther islands. We huddled, while the waves rolled by and the boat rose, heaved and sank in the grey-green swell.

The Pinnacle Rocks were dark with rain when we passed; sea-birds fluttered and swooped; the air full of their cries. Herring gulls and terns clustered thickly on each ledge and on top of the cliffs, shining white on those black fangs.

We landed on the Longstone, bare but for its lighthouse and wild with wind and rain and gulls; their short cries came fitfully in gusts. Longstone is nothing but a rock, but in the mating season bird eggs lie scattered about on strands of seaweed. We stumbled along the ledges looking for nests, slipping on pods of kelp, the briny pungence of the place in our nostrils all the time.

I crept along to the edge of the rock, and lying down there peered over to watch the heaped-up waves and spindrift that swirled below. The spray blew up into my face and the boom of the water beat on my ears. I remembered that St. Cuthbert had lived on one of these islands for years in solitude. Surely he must have sometimes longed to be out of the swing of the sea. Part of his chapel still stands in this desolate place; perhaps communing with his saints and angels, he never found it lonely. But at other times, surely, he must've looked from his cell at night towards the shore and saw with longing the dark hills where once he'd been a shepherd-boy.

ON THE LAST DAY at Barmoor before going South, I found poor Miss

Turnbull almost in tears at the thought of our going. I went out in the afternoon to get away from household things, the packing and mending of the boys' clothes before they went off back to school. Directly I enter the path with the beech trees on either side, that leads down to the Moss Wood, my spirits lift and all weariness deserts me. It really is an ecstacy for me to be there, my very own ecstacy, not connected so much with outside things; the colour, the scent, the softness of the earth.

The next morning we started off with the customary farewells; the men at the door, the Henrys at the gates of the East Lodge, Miss Turnbull waving madly from her cottage.

The journey itself was pleasant enough, except for sparring between Bill and Simon. I was so pleased to be among my dear Cockneys again. We drove from Kings Cross to Grosvenor Road in a small bus; the driver wished us all a prosperous New Year. How different to the silent, expressionless North; it warmed my heart.

Poor Willie doesn't enjoy London very much, I fear. He liked taking the boys to the Science Museum though. We went to St Martins on Sundays and every week to Chatham House. One day we heard Lord Cecil talking about disarmament. What a noble creature, how I do admire him; seeing his face and feeling that not one petty thought can be found in him. He was so amusing too, so self-less in his endeavours. What a glorious representative for this country to have at the League of Nations. May he live for year and years.

People always came to our house in Grosvenor Road. They liked its position: the way it looked straight onto the river with its never-ending activity. On the far side of the river, directly opposite, the Battersea power station was being built. It fascinated me to see the way the framework altered from visit to visit. The boys loved watching the tugs with their barges going up and down, and ships carrying coal twice a week from the North of England to the gas works farther up the river, but the boys liked *Mr Therm* the best; I believe it belonged to the Gas Light and Coke Company. When it went under the railway bridge carrying the trains from Victoria to the South coast, its whole funnel was lowered flat. Everyone rushed to the window just in case someone forgot and it hit the railway bridge. What horror and delight might have been.

I felt so surrounded by friends in London. Life was simpler, one could meet people all the time, talk to them on the telephone and arrange to see them. Hardly a day passed without a luncheon.

Without our house in Grosvenor Road, we wouldn't have seen so much of Bill at Harrow and Simon at Winchester. Both were quickly reachable. To my surprise, I didn't find it difficult to get on with my book too. My drawing-room upstairs didn't compare with the oval room at Barmoor, but I was much more at peace with myself, not cut off from friends. The years went by. Life was still wonderful to me, just as much as it used to be, though I did feel sometimes that I could see forward towards the end now.

In the last few weeks of 1931, the doctors grew worried about Willie. The fear that he might die before long made me want to draw nearer to God, to be more alive and aware of a greater reality. I wanted to be more moulded, more formed by his indwelling spirit. Eternal life, here and now, I wanted to understand it at last and firmly hold onto it.

How shall I write it? It happened days ago but it still seems so strange that my darling Willie is gone from me; he has left me after twenty years. I've had his faithfulness, never changing, and those darling blue eyes, which gazed till the last. I can't stare at them anymore. I was never able to look at them without tears, when he came to see me off at the station, and now —

Willie, darling! Darling, where are you? Am I still your sweetheart, your precious? I love you so. Do you know how much?

I'd gone to say goodnight to him; he seemed very exhausted and weak. The nurse had given me brandy to make me sleep but just after midnight I heard a car and jumped out of bed. I went to his room and saw my sweet, beloved Willie propped up, looking bluer than before and breathing noisily. Even I could see he was dying.

I sat as near to him as I could and held his dear hand. First, he was so hot and then he grew cold. The doctor came and sat on the other side of the bed. I said some prayers for my beloved; I kissed and kissed him on the forehead. I whispered that one kiss was from Ann, one from Bill, and one from Simon, and with the sign of the cross, I marked his forehead and over his heart.

I watched him go slowly; all the love in the world couldn't keep him. He breathed slower and slower, quite unconscious, and then he stopped, and left me alone. All those years together, how much he had loved me as a girl; he was mine alone then.

The doctor spoke. "He is free now, he is free."

I said I didn't want to leave him and lay on the bed by his dear side until they made me go. The doctor came into the drawing-room with me and said how Willie was still there and that if we were more sensitive we could probably see him if we weren't so encrusted. The doctor was so kind, he fortified me. "Perhaps you will see him sooner than you think," he said. I thanked him very much; I was so dazed. I went up to my room and looked out of the window at the shining stars and wondered where Willie might be.

ALL THIS WEEK, the national feeling of crisis became stronger and stronger; I listened on the wireless to Mr Chamberlain's speech to the House of Commons, which was marvellously united with only four dissidents. Then I heard Lord Halifax with his nice calm voice and no heroics of any sort; what a comfort after the German and Italian style. He was broadcast to the United States. The Dominions, Canada and Australia are responding wonderfully, but the crisis is increasing. The Pope also has made a broadcast for peace and Mr Roosevelt has sent a message to the King of Italy, which seems rather pointless.

That August, back at Barmoor, the house was full of people. Bill and Simon worked at the Home Farm, helping paint and white-wash the buildings. Susan Elwes and, later, her sister Nancy came to stay and were persuaded to work as well, and Roddy Lambton came over from Fenton nearly every day to amuse us all.

On Simon's birthday, he and I walked to the garden after tea to pick raspberries and talk. We agreed what a difference it made to believe in a richer life beyond, and that if anything did happen to him, should war begin, that darling Willie would be waiting above. Simon believed this true absolutely, I'm sure, which was an enormous comfort to me. He was only nineteen and the thought, that he might not have much longer to live, was quite unbearable.

Only two weeks later, the supremely awful did happen. War did start again. The wireless this morning said that the Germans had bombed Warsaw and crossed the frontier, causing a tremendous sense of excitement and horror. At eleven, came the announcement, for all Territorials to report at six that evening.

Simon put on his uniform and went to the drill hall at Lowick; the first to arrive, he was told he needn't have come until nine. After dinner Bill drove me down to Lowick where a crowd waited to see the contingent off. It was a half-exalted, half-tragic scene. Poor Mrs Gibson stood there crying with her wretched crippled son at her side with his crutches. Mr Nichol, the schoolmaster, went into the drill hall and talked to all the Lowick boys. They cheered him and sang songs.

It was a warm, dark night. Simon came and held my hand and kissed me. His friend, Harry Gibson, shook my other hand. Lots of the mothers were in tears and as their boys drove off into the night the whole village cheered. Bill and I returned home; neither of us spoke; we knew things had changed irrevocably.

NEARLY TWELVE YEARS have passed since Willie died and here I am, alone in this enormous house, with all its rooms empty, sitting on the old red sofa in the library, with the memories of thirty years crowding upon me; Those rooms have echoed to so many steps, so much talk, such callings and rushings of children.

It is October 1943 and another war is raging, but the troops which were billeted here have, for the time being, gone; and the quiet of their sudden absence is wonderful.

The fire is piled with both logs and coal and there are pine cones to toss on as well. I burnt some dry rosemary twigs a little time ago and the spicy fragrance of it lingers in the air.

I've been looking out of the window, idly reflecting. Outside, the early sun warms everything with its pleasant glow; the beds of snapdragons encircle the pond. The flowers, crimson, saffron and coral, burnish the yellow bronze of autumn leaves and brighten the fields. I can see the low line of hills along the Tweed. Deep silence is overall.

The house, too, is deeply still; as if time itself has stopped to let the past flow back in all its fullness. In this solitude, which way shall I turn the eyes of my mind? Which scene shall I call up from the inexhaustible well of other years?

Here we are bound to this tiny conscious fragment of ourselves, here on this rolling earth is imperfect memory; but beyond there is liberty and completion where we will inherit the treasures now collected. This beautiful world, which is almost weighed down with its wealth of life, is full with wonder.

Should I live to be very old, with no letters or luncheons expected of me, I'd give one day up to the memory of each friend, each separate prized encounter. I will shut my eyes to this dear English room and the leaping flames and see only the rocky ground of Boluchistan with tall eremurus and tulips springing up from the harsh earth; see the jagged mountains, little spinneys full of grape-hyacinths; and across the plains, the black and white lambs, the striped tents, the glorious-looking Boluchis working the land, clad in scarlet velvet waistcoats and full white trousers.

After the oval room, the green drawing-room, now a sick bay for the Army, I love the library dearest of all. The children came to it often: Ann and Bill in their scarlet pinafores and glowing cheeks and curls, and Simon, a sour-faced little one with his yellow hair cut in a fringe. Where are they now, I wonder? Clad in very different clothes, with Bill in the Navy and Simon in the Air Force.

The library is piled high with family photograph books, travel diaries, and masses of letters received from early youth onwards.

But now it grows dark; only the firelight is left; the sunset is over, but I must still walk through the 65 rooms of the house in the fading light, drawing the black out curtains. Tomorrow, perhaps, when the present is not so insistent, I will look through an old batch of letters and live again that year.

Sadly our lovely house in Grosvenor Road was blitzed. When the war is over, I'll move to a smaller one in Victoria Square, close to Gorringes, with Warren, an old-fashioned grocer, at the corner.

Simon, living near Horsham and travelling up and down every day to his office in the City, drops in regularly once a week to see me. Bill wrote to me from Barmoor quite often but didn't come South much; when he did appear, he seemed to spend most of his time with Campbell Cotts and their actress friend, Penelope. He never talked about her; perhaps he was too embarrassed after the way he'd behaved towards Anna. Ann told me that he was very hard up but I didn't believe her; he gave me such glowing reports of his lime-crushing business and how well it was doing.

Simon, on a Wednesday visit in London, told me differently. He appeared very downcast and pre-occupied in his neat blue suit and polished black shoes.

"I don't think Bill's doing at all well," said Simon gloomily. This was Simon at his worst. I found him quite exasperating when he went on and on about things in his laborious way. I tried to change the subject. "I suppose you'll be going abroad again soon on one of your business trips, won't you?" I asked.

He sat there silently. Then he nodded.

"Cheer up, darling. Here, have a little more sherry."

He shook his head. How yellow his hair was still! And those strange greeny-blue eyes. I remembered him still in dress uniform. I liked him better then. I like Edith least of all now. She told me to stop using the Sitwell name for my books. How can she say such a thing? She's Simon's godmother.

Simon

141

CONSEQUENCES

A JOURNEY NORTH

Simon threw his overnight bag into the corner of his office and rang for his secretary. "Good morning, Ruth. Will you ask Miss Woodman if I can see Mr Peyton-Jones right away?"

He pulled the chair up to the desk and looked at his diary. The trip to Drammen in Norway had to be put off, if possible; he had better ring them up and talk to them. Reaching into his pocket, he pulled out an envelope; on the back he'd scribbled a few notes coming up in the fast train that morning.

His secretary came back into the room. "Mr Peyton-Jones will see you now, sir."

"Try to get me on the 1.20 train from Kings Cross to Berwick, please, Ruth. And will you ask Mr Martens if he can go instead of me to see the Bruusgaards in the middle of the week?"

The secretary began writing in her notebook. Simon frowned.

"Hang on; get me a return ticket to Newcastle, not Berwick; and arrange for a self-drive car to be at the station."

The girl nodded. "Will you be away for long?" she asked.

"Only a day or two, I hope." He got up and went through to the next door office, the managing director's room.

"Come in, Sammy. What's the trouble?" Then turning to his secretary, he said: "Be a dear and bring us some coffee, would you, Woodpecker?" Good old Jeremy, thought Simon. When it came to pure charm he was superb. "What's the trouble, old boy?"

Simon took a moment to collect his thoughts. He'd momentarily allowed himself to think about the *Carslogie*. Being called Sammy always took him back to those days at sea less than twenty years before. "I've got to go up to Barmoor. It's urgent," he said.

"Why? Has it burnt down, or something?"

Simon gave a brief account of what had happened.

"Christ!" Jeremy looked genuinely dismayed. "What a bloody awful state of affairs. Hasn't your family's been there for ages?"

Jeremy and Simon were distantly related, through the Talbots and the Grosvenors, but until their paths crossed in business, they had never met. Yet, Simon dimly remembered him being in the

Eton boxing team when they'd drawn against Harrow in public schools competition.

"About two hundred years, I suppose," Simon answered. "Is it okay if I go up there this afternoon?"

"Of course. What did you have planned for this week?"

"A trip to Drammen. Bruusgaards want to talk to me about their new-building, the Hallvard. Peter Martens can go in my place; he's just as capable as I am."

"Alright. I'll have a word with Bill Pritchard-Gordon and ask him to keep an eye on the telexes. Good luck, old boy. Let me know if I can help at all."

Sitting in the train, Simon reflected how lucky he was to be working for such a staunch ally. Jeremy was a tough businessman but would do anything for his friends. With his slightly pugilistic face, he didn't fit the conventional Old Etonian image.

I expect the war changed him a lot, thought Simon. Jeremy had been with a West African regiment and seen quite a bit of active service in the Far East. Someone said he'd ended up as a Colonel.

A car was waiting for Simon at Newcastle and he was soon on his way up the Great North road. Past Gosforth, Morpeth and Alnwick; what familiar names. He hadn't imagined that he'd see them again in these circumstances.

As it was too late to call in at Barmoor, he went straight to Lennel. That morning he'd telephoned Betty and asked if she could put him up for a few nights. Despite the breakdown of her marriage to Bill, Simon had kept on good terms with her, and his wife and children had been to see her over the years.

Now, sitting in the same room, where he'd visited to retrieve his brother's suits, he faced Betty again, but he wasn't nervous of her any more. He'd decided that she was a kind, helpful woman, outspoken but free of bitterness or resentment, and furthermore, extremely intelligent.

"What on earth are you doing up here?" she asked.

"Bill's disappeared and I'm told the place is up for sale."

"That doesn't surprise me," she answered coolly. "The way he's been carrying on, I'm not in the least shocked."

She drew on her cigarette.

"What d'you mean, carrying on?" Simon asked.

"All these actresses and people who've moved in, it seems. I'm told they have all-night parties and Bill isn't seen for days. How on earth does he think he can run things, living like that?"

"Good point," murmured Simon.

"I've never met any of them except for Campbell Cotts. He's been there a lot, I believe."

Simon sighed. "Ever since Bill sold Brackenside, I thought it might come to this. But I never thought he'd do a bunk."

"Silly ass."

"I agree."

"You know, umpteen people up here would've helped him. Like Claude Lambton and Jock Askew; he was very popular."

Simon nodded. "Well, it's too late now. I probably won't see you in the morning; I'll have to get going as soon as I can." he added.

"That's alright, darling. D'you want to borrow a car?"

"No thanks; I've got one."

Later that evening, as he switched off the light by his bed, he thanked God for his kind and generous friends.

Crossman Bolam looked at Simon over the top of his glasses and remarked, "Aye, Simon. A bad business; a very bad business. Dieu knows what your father would have made of it all."

Bolam's office in Hyde Hill was a familiar landmark in Berwick. Simon sat quietly. Bolam's idiomatic voice had always fascinated him. Saying Dieu instead of God was quite common on the Borders but he hadn't heard it used for years. "I can't tell you a lot," Bolam continued. " Your brother and I saw less and less of each other; he didn't come in every week like the General."

"But you're still the agent, aren't you?"

"For the estate, yes. But then all these other things are going on; I never knew what was what. The only wages I saw to were for the estate workers; not the men on the sawmill or at the quarry. Mind you, I knew a lot of timber felling went on. Reavley and Mr Jack were in here quite often complaining about the fences and gates."

"Fences and gates?"

"Aye. They're always being damaged by the big lorries leading the timber."

"And I suppose they were never mended?"

"That's right," said Mr Bolam gloomily.

"Then there was that business over Brackenside; I'm told the Mill Farm has gone too."

"What!" exclaimed Simon.

"Yes; he sold the Mill Farm to Forsyth. Did ye not know?" Mr Bolam stayed in his chair shaking his head. "Aye, it's a bad, bad business, Simon. The family sent you up here, did they?"

"No, not really. Thomson telephoned me with the news."

"There's not much I can do to help, I'm afraid. Have you any idea how bad it is?"

"Not until I see Mr Carmichael, the bank manager."

"When will you be seeing him then?" asked Mr Bolam.

"In about ten minutes. I'm going out to Barmoor after lunch."

"D'you want me to come with you?"

"No thanks, Crossie; thanks all the same. I'll telephone you in the morning to let you know what I've found."

"Mr Carmichael won't tell you anything, Simon."

Mr Bolam was looking gloomier than ever.

You're probably right, but I've got to try."

Simon got up and left the old-fashioned office. Mr Lindsay, Bolam's chief clerk, stood at the top of the stairs.

"It's nice to see you again, Mr Simon." They shook hands.

"I must be getting along, I've got a busy day," Simon said and hurried down Hide Hill and through the doors of Barclays Bank.

Crossie Bolam was right. Mr Carmichael was friendly but, he explained, his hands were tied. "I'd like to help you, Mr Sitwell; I really would. But I have to respect the confidences of my clients." He sighed and looked at Simon, a wan expression on his face.

"But, surely, you can stretch a point, can't you? I've come a long way to try and help; can't you bend the rules a little?"

"That's impossible." After a long silence, Mr Carmichael leant forward over his desk. "I shouldn't be telling you this but you should be seeing the Agricultural Mortgage Corporation."

"That's very good of you, Mr Carmichael; but do you think they'll tell me anything? Won't their hands be tied as well?"

"Aye, I daresay," said Mr Carmichael, lapsing into Border talk. "They'll not ken to you unless you hold a Power of Attorney from your brother; same as me."

"I thought as much."

"Aye, the best thing you can do, Mr Sitwell, is to get a proper Power of Attorney drawn up, and have your brother sign it."

The bank manager relaxed back in his chair, pleased that he'd been able to bring the meeting to an end. "Aye, that's what you want to do; get a Power of Attorney signed. Then you'll be able to look at the books, open his letters; see the creditors, doubtless."

Simon got up. They shook hands.

"I'll be pleased to meet with you at any time, Mr Sitwell; but mind you get that authority."

"Easier said than done. How do I get him to sign something when I don't even know where he is?"

"Well, I wish you luck, Mr Sitwell. All I can tell you is that your brother is in very serious trouble."

Simon nodded, shrugged his shoulders and left, wondering if he still had time to get a quick bite to eat.

At Barmoor, getting out of the hired car, he could hear the high-pitched moan of the saw as it laboured at the mill with the limbs of the freshly-cut trees.

Half the lawn was already in shadow, the sunlight cut off by the tall battlements of the Castle. The white garden chairs were still in their usual place by the huge rhododendron bush; the grass looked neat and recently cut and some rabbits were nibbling away at the corner of the lawn where it merged with the path leading to the kitchen garden.

Simon walked through the stable yard to Thomson's house and knocked on the door.

"Hullo, Thomson; I came as quickly as I could."

Thomson stood on the doorstep. What a familiar sight; the same old brown boiler suit; the pipe in his mouth. The door of his house had been freshly painted. Simon wondered, idly, what had prompted that desperate last-minute face-lift. Had Bill had it done or had Thomson in a last defiant gesture, ordered the paint from the estate office and painted it himself?

"You're looking well, Master Simon."

Simon smiled as they shook hands.

"You'd better come in. You'll have a cup of tea, will ye not?

They talked for the next hour.

"If ye want to see Jimmy, ye'd better go, Master Simon," said Thomson, glancing at his old kitchen clock. Jimmy was his younger son who ran the sawmill.

""I'll be over again in the morning then." Simon said and walked down to the sawmill. Half-a-dozen men were getting ready to leave on their bicycles. They touched their caps to Simon.

"Where's Jimmy?" asked Simon.

"He's round at the back, Master Simon."

Jimmy approached him wiping his hands on an oily rag. Many's the time they had bombarded each other during the pre-war fir-cone battles in Dunsall wood. "I heard you were on the way up, Master Simon," he said.

"When did you last see Mr Bill?" Simon asked.

"He was down seeing the lads on the Thursday. Aye, it'd be the Thursday."

"What did he tell you?"

"He said he'd be away for a while, that I was just to carry on."

"Carry on running the sawmill? What about the wages and the stamps and things? Who would pay you?"

Jimmy looked sheepish. "He just said to go on as usual and pay ourselves out of the money which came in."

"Is there any money coming in?"

"Not a lot, Master Simon. We've sent a few loads of pitprop lids away to the N.C.B. Mr Bill said we was to ask for cash for them."

"Is there any money over to pay for diesel fuel for the engine?"

Jimmy pulled a face. "Hardly. Put it this way, Master Simon; we can just about keep going; but there's no money over."

Simon shook his head and looked at the ground. "I'll talk to Mr

Bolam but you'll have to close down; probably at the end of next week. You'd better tell the men."

Jimmy looked crestfallen. "Have you no news of Mr Bill then?"

"I'm afraid not."

"What's going to happen?"

"Dieu knows. What about you, Jimmy? Can you get your old job back?" Jimmy had worked at Foreman's, the Lowick bakers.

"I'll have to try; the wife's expecting."

"I'm very sorry, Jimmy. I'll see if I can think of something but I'm not hopeful." They shook hands. "I'll be over in the morning again; maybe I'll see you then?"

Driving back to Coldstream, Simon reflected on the day. He'd always disapproved of cutting down trees, but just to keep the sawmill working without any profit at the end was crazy. It was only a matter of time before there were no more trees and the mill had to stop anyway. "I think Bill must've gone off his head," he said to Betty when they met later.

They sat in front of the fire after dinner, with the dogs lying all over the place, as usual, occupying the most comfortable chairs.

"I must say, I think it's very awkward for you, darling."

"I know; I've got no authority. I haven't really got the right to close down the sawmill. Bolam will have to do it, even though he doesn't have anything to do with that side of the estate."

"What a ghastly mess."

"I'll go over in the morning and get the night train down from Newcastle. I've got to hand back the car there, anyway."

"Next time you come up, I'll have you met off the train at Berwick. We'll be able to lend you a car."

"Thanks awfully." One of the dogs got up and scratched at the curtains covering the window of the garden door. "I'll let them out, if you like; then I'd better go to bed."

"See you when you're next up; I'm sure it won't be more than a week or two," said Betty.

Simon left her looking into the fire. In bed, he could hear the faint barking of the dogs in the garden outside.

At Barmoor again, on his morning visit, Simon saw the quarry deserted. Lorries and spreader trucks stood about looking as if they'd been abandoned. An air of desolation hung over the place, the power house padlocked, puddles of water filling the ruts made by the heavy equipment. The plant had obviously not worked for some time; presumably his brother had laid off the men here.

In the Castle, piles of unopened letters lay around. Simon wandered the rooms trying to recall what they'd looked like and what was missing. A painting here and there seemed to have been removed but the silver, what he could remember of it, was intact.

There wasn't time to do much and, in any case, technically he was trespassing until he had a valid Power of Attorney.

On returning to London he got in touch with Hugo Southern, one of the partners in Frere Cholmeley, the family's lawyers.

"I'll have a suitable document drawn up and post it to you in the next few days," Hugo said and assured Simon that if he could have it signed by his brother and witnessed, it would enable him to deal with all Bill's affairs and find out fully what was happening.

A week passed and Thomson telephoned. Scrap-merchants had been round asking if they could buy the sawmill machinery.

"You mustn't sell anything, Thomson. It's not ours to sell."

"Have ye any word from Mr Bill?"

"No." But the next day, Simon got a call from his mother while he was in his office. "I've had a letter from Bill, darling."

"Go ahead; what does it say?"

"He's back at sea; the letter's posted from Halifax."

Does he say what ship he's on?"

"The *S.S. Cairngowan*; that's what it looks like."

"Hang on, Mama; I'll look her up. I think she's one of Cairns Nobles; wait a minute."

A moment or two later, Simon picked up the telephone. "Yes, I've found her; does he give an address?"

"Care of Furness Withy, London."

"Yes, that's her. I'll ring you in a day or two."

It didn't take Simon long to find out what he needed to know; Furness Withy's office was just across the road from his.

"She'll be docking at Middlesbrough in ten days' time. She's on our liner service from the U.K and Continent to Canada."

On his next Wednesday call to his mother in Victoria Square, Simon asked her not to go away the following week, as the ship would be docking Tuesday next.

"What are you planning to do, darling?" she asked.

"I'll let you know on Monday." No point telling her anything yet; she might let the cat out of the bag.

"Will you try to see him? Perhaps he'll come to London?"

"I doubt it."

"Oh, don't be so gloomy, darling; can't you ever look on the bright side? I'm sure he'll come and see me."

"I'll ring you up on Monday; mind you're here," Simon said.

That weekend, Simon set his strategy. Hugo Southern had sent him the blank Power of Attorney. All that remained was to get his brother's signature. He telephoned his mother on Monday. "I'm coming round in a taxi for you tomorrow at 2.15; pack a few things as we'll be away for the night."

"What? Why?"

"Mama," said Simon wearily. "Please, do as I ask; we're going away for a night; I'll tell you all on the train."

"What about tickets and things?"

"I'll have them; just be ready when I come round."

Ruth, his secretary, made arrangements. "I don't know what the hotel's like; there's not a big selection in Darlington," she said.

On Tuesday, he collected his mother. Once they were on board, his mother's mood changed. "It's ages since you and I were in a train together, darling. D'you remember how you always made me take you to look at the engine?"

"Yes, I still go and have a look. It won't be long before they've gone to diesel." Simon hated the transition away from steam. Beeching and Co must be mad, scrapping all those engines; they had years of life left in them. The Germans, whom he admired when it came to business, planned to keep all their main-line steam engines for years to come.

But his mother had other things on her mind.

"What will happen tomorrow? You haven't told me yet."

"We'll be seeing Bill; his ship's alongside at Middlesbrough. We want him to sign that paper."

"What paper?"

Simon explained. "We can't come back to London without his signature; otherwise the whole thing will be a waste of time."

"D'you think he'll sign?"

"I shouldn't think so; he'll say he wants time to think."

"Well, darling, if he won't sign it, he won't sign it. I don't know what we can do."

"He's got to sign it; there's no other way to save the situation."

"But d'you think it's as bad as all that?"

"Yes, but I don't know how bad. Nobody will tell me anything. I'm not allowed to see his bank balances; nobody knows how much money he owes. No one can do anything without his authority and that bit of paper I gave you to read, Mama, gives the authority."

"Well, I'll do my best, darling."

The train gathered speed, galloping across the fens of Lincolnshire. "Let's get a cup of tea," said Simon, on arriving.

The docks were deserted; so far, the plan was working. The train from Darlington to Middlesbrough had come in at midday. Simon knew that the ship gangs had knocked off for their dinner. It was not that long ago that he'd been a messroom boy in the *Carslogie*. With a bit of luck, the crew of the *Cairngowan* would be having their dinner also when he and his mother finally got on board.

He clutched her arm, steering her round the railway wagons and cranes which seemed to be everywhere. "Is that the ship?" she asked. Simon glanced to where she was pointing. The *Cairngowan* looked enormous, her sides rising high from the dockside. To his dismay he saw that the bottom of the gangway was four feet above the quay. As if to read his thoughts, his mother asked him how they were going to get on board.

"Here, hold this." He handed her his bag.

"What are you going to do, darling?"

"I'm going to try and get onto it and lower it down."

"Oh, do be careful!"

The task reminded him of the gym at Harrow. Pull-ups at the

bar; the endless practising to try and get into the gym eight level class. Now, aged thirty-six, it wasn't quite so easy.

"Give me a push, Ma," he said, finding himself in a struggle to get his feet up. Successful, he ran up the gangway and lowered away. The decks of the ship were deserted, with no one to witness the bizarre invasion by a city slicker and an aristocratic old lady. "Christ knows what anyone would think if they were watching," Simon mused. "Just typical that the bloody gangway would be halfway up the side of the ship."

Once up the gangway ladder, they reached the well deck aft. How familiar it was; ships didn't change. "Don't talk, just follow me," Simon muttered. He knew where to make for; the mess would be at the end of the portside alleyway. "Wait here."

Simon walked slowly down the alleyway, hearing the sound of the officers as they took their dinner break. A white-coated steward came round the corner. "Can I help you, sir?"

"The third mate; is his name Sitwell?"

"Aye." The man looked puzzled.

"Fetch him. Don't tell him anything; just say he's wanted outside." Simon pressed a pound note into the man's hand and gave him a wink.

As the man went back, Simon beckoned to his mother. "You stand here." He moved her inside the alleyway, to the corner of the dining saloon. Positioning himself behind her, he placed his hand on her shoulder. "Bill's in there; you'll see him in a second."

Before she could say anything, Bill came round the corner.

"Mama! Good Lord!" Bill's face went white; Simon thought Bill was going to faint.

They embraced each other. "We'd better go up to my cabin." They followed him up the stairs. "Have you had some lunch? I can get you sandwiches if you like."

'I wonder what the hell he's thinking,' thought Simon, making himself comfortable on the bunk settee. He could've been back on the *Carslogie*, it was all so familiar. 'We must've given Bill a hell of a shock. Still, since he shoved off as he had, he had to put up with the consequences.'

"You're not to worry, darling," said his mother. " We're not here to scold you or anything; we want to help. Simon's got a document for you to sign."

Bill glared at his brother, as if to say, 'Interfering little bastard; poking your nose in again as usual.'

Aloud he said: "What document?"

"It's a Power of Attorney, Bill." Simon, confronted with that look of hate, felt his resolve disappearing.

"What the hell's a power of attorney?"

"It enables me to act for you."

"Why should I want you to act for me? Anyone would think I wasn't of age or something."

Simon took a deep breath and glanced at his mother.

"Why don't we leave Ma here and go somewhere else to talk?" he said firmly and sighed to himself.

"Okay. We'll go onto the bridge; won't be long, Ma."

Once up there, they began to walk backwards and forwards. It was a bit like the old days except that the bridge of the *Cairngowan* was considerably less roomy than the east drive at Barmoor, their favourite pre-war rendezvous. "Christ, the lead on the roof must be worth a fortune!" exclaimed Bill.

"I daresay it is," agreed Simon. " But that won't pay the bills."

"That bloody bank manager," said Bill, his voice harsh with bitterness. "All over you one minute; then, wham! Bastards."

Simon nodded. He'd have to go along with him if he was ever to get the form signed. "I know."

"They just suddenly pulled down the shutters," went on his brother. "Bastards, that's what they are: bloody bastards."

Simon looked at his watch. If they were to get back to London that night he'd better try and speed things up.

"Look, Bill, you think I'm so bloody clever; well, let me tell you something; I'm not." Simon paused. Bill stared out of the side window at the other ships in the dock.

"Go on, then," his brother scoffed.

Simon could sense the hostility and suspicion, but continued, "I've made the most almighty balls-ups, you know; everyone does."

"So you've made some balls-ups," Bill replied sarcastically.

"All I mean is that you're not the only one, that's all," Simon concluded lamely.

"Got anything else to say?"

Simon shook his head.

"Well, let's go below and see Ma. Who's bright idea was it anyway, coming up here like this? You could have let me know."

"Never mind; it was mine actually, not that it matters very much," Simon said bitterly.

When they entered the cabin, their mother was reading *Light*, a spiritualist magazine. She looked up.

"I don't think Bill wants to sign that form," said Simon.

"I want to think about it."

Simon gave his mother a look; it was now or never.

"Oh, I think I'd sign it if I were you, darling. You're so busy and you'll be going back to sea in a few days; why not let Simon take care of things?"

"I'd like to think about it."

"You can always revoke it , you know," said Simon. Anything to get the damned thing agreed.

"Well, let me have another look at it," muttered his brother.

"Go on, darling," cajoled his mother, sensing that the time had come to put her spoke in.

"No, I'd like to read it through properly. I'll let you know."

"Why don't you just sign it, please, darling?" persevered his mother. "Look, I've got a pen somewhere. I'll see that Simon does not do anything silly."

Simon held his breath.

"Alright, lend me your pen," Bill said and signed his name.

"Is there someone we can get to witness it?" asked Simon. "Anyone will do; why don't you get the steward?"

Bill got up and went to the door. A man appeared wearing a white jacket.

"Would you mind witnessing this, Mick?"

The man signed his name clumsily. Simon could hardly believe it. "If we want the fast train back, we'd better be off," he said.

Bill followed to the top of the gangway and watched them as they made their way across the busy dock, now bustling with fork-lift trucks and stevedores. They waved to each other.

"Well done, Griper," said Simon to his mother.

She looked at her son. He hadn't used that nickname for her since he'd been a little boy.

SIMON SAT on the floor of the smoking-room at Barmoor. Around him, heaped in little piles, were reports, letters and unpaid bills.

Two months had passed since the encounter with his brother on the *Cairngowan*. With the Power of Attorney he'd been to Barmoor twice, seen Bill's bankers, his solicitors, and felt sufficiently informed to tackle the biggest creditor, the Agricultural Mortgage Corporation.

David Gavin, a colleague of Simon's at Clarksons, had helped arrange for him to see one of the top men there. It wasn't hard to realize what had to be done to save Bill from bankruptcy. All Simon had done so far was total up the amount due to creditors, add on the unpaid bills and put the final figure against the amount held by his brother and the estate. Apart from some rents due, there was no set-off at all. Bill was broke, unless he had funds elsewhere that Simon didn't know about. The Mortgage Corporation had been very courteous and sympathetic.

"I've looked at the file and see that there are at least two repayments overdue and another imminent," Simon said. He did his best to look relaxed and confident. The two men in the room with him shuffled their papers before answering.

"Yes, Mr Sitwell. There's a substantial amount of interest due, not to mention the capital sum outstanding."

Simon nodded.

"Your brother agreed that we should have a charge on the farms as security for the loan."

"Yes?"

The men looked at him questioningly. "To get to the point, Mr Sitwell; how does your brother intend to repay that money?"

"There'll be a sale of some of his assets," Simon said, prepared.

The two men glanced at each other. One leant forward and peered over his glasses. "Those assets must be substantial; the amount outstanding is not small by any standard. We want to be helpful, but you should realise that we do insist on repayment."

"When?" Simon asked.

"Now, Mr Sitwell; now! We can't let the debt run on and have the interest pile up; we have to look after our company's finances."

Here we go, thought Simon. He took a deep breath. "In other words, you'll have to foreclose?" he asked.

"I'm afraid so; we had a valuation done of the farms and we think we are covered satisfactorily."

"I'm not so sure about that; none of them are in hand."

"We know that."

"By the time you add on the interest, it could be a close thing."

There was a silence.

"I'd like an extension and a moratorium on the debt interest," said Simon suddenly.

"How long had you in mind?"

"Three or four months."

"That's asking a lot."

"Maybe it is; but I must have time."

"Why will it take you so long?"

"Because, like you, I have to earn a living. I'm in London, I work full-time and can only deal with the Barmoor estate at weekends. As it is, I come up every month." Simon paused to see what effect his remarks were having. The men sat there. One of them tapped with his pencil on the desk.

"It's a long way to go; not like going down to Bexhill-on-Sea or somewhere like that," Simon added.

The shadow of a smile came over the face of one of them.

"We'll talk it over; maybe we'll be able to bend the rules a bit."

"Thanks. If you leave it to me, you've every chance of getting your money back plus interest; and it won't cost you as much as arranging a forced sale."

They all stood up. "You've got a point there, Mr Sitwell. Forced sales never make very good prices."

ON ONE VISIT to see his mother, Simon found his sister there.

"What's happening up at Barmoor?" Ann asked.

Their mother sat in her chair by the window, gazing out over the square. That the subject had been brought up irritated her. There they were, the three of them, with her dying to hear about her grandchildren and this wretched business had to be discussed again. She was sick to death of it. "Do we really have to talk about this today?" she grumbled.

"I'd much rather talk about something else," Simon answered. "You needn't think I particularly enjoy going up there all the time; I practically have to wear a disguise to avoid the creditors."

"Are there a lot of them?" asked his sister.

"Yes, I'm afraid there are."

"But you'll be able to pay them in the end, won't you?" said his mother. She still couldn't believe it was as bad as Simon made out. 'I believe he rather enjoys his role,' she thought to herself. 'Always looking on the black side of things.'

"Oh, do cheer up, darling," she said, smiling. "I can always let you have a little money; some of my shares are doing marvellously."

"Sorry, Mama."

"Have you managed to sell any of the farms yet?" asked Ann.

"I've had a lot of help from Basil Greenwell."

"Isn't he Damian's godfather? I've heard you talking about him before; he lives near you in Sussex, doesn't he? Does he know a lot about this sort of thing then?"

"Yes, he's a senior partner in Strutt and Parker; of course he does." Even Ann, with her lack of business savoir-faire, must have heard of them, thought Simon. "There are only three farms left to sell," he added, answering her original question.

"Well, they must be worth a lot, aren't they, darling?" asked his mother reassuringly.

"They would have been if Bill and Crossie Bolam had listened to me." Simon still felt bitter that his advice had been disregarded. Under the new Act, the existing tenants were protected for life. He wasn't sure, but he believed the tenancy even passed on to the eldest son on the death of the tenant farmer. "I'm told that I'll do best by selling the farms to the tenants, because no one else wants to buy land with a fixed tenant on it."

"I'll come up with you if you like, when you go again?" Ann said.

"Thanks awfully. You can help me list all the silver and put it away. I've had it insured but I'll take it to the bank; we can't just leave it in an empty house."

"Can we stay in the house? What's it like?"

"Parts of it smell very damp and the roof leaks above the top schoolroom." He'd a hunch, parts of the roof were affected by dry rot. No point in saying anything; he could see that his mother was becoming more and more tight-lipped. If he went on bearing more tidings of woe, she'd lose her temper. He looked at his watch.

"I'll have to go in a minute."

"Let me know when you've fixed a date." said Ann.

"Okay. Goodbye, Mama. See you next week." He kissed her and left the house. That night, Simon discussed the day's events with his wife. Before long, inevitably, the subject of Barmoor came up.

"What's going to happen to it?"

"God knows!" said Simon sadly. The whole thing was getting him down. These everlasting visits to Northumberland. Without Betty he wouldn't have managed. At least he was comfortable there and able to get around in the car she always gave him.

"D'you think Bill will ever live there again?" asked Simon's wife.

"Assuming we're able to save it, there's nothing to stop him; but he'll never be able to keep it up."

"Perhaps he'll get a job?"

"What at? The only thing he knows about is running a ship."

"I wouldn't mind living there if it were smaller and modernised. We could perhaps share it with Ann and James for the holidays."

"It's worth a thought," said Simon. "But there's a lot to see to before we begin to think about it."

"You could talk to Ann when you're there with her; she's very fond of the place; we'd buy it jointly, if we could persuade Bill to sell to us; James is doing quite well. I could talk to my trustees. We'd leave it to the children then; make a trust so it always stayed in the family," Phoebette went on, with persistent enthusiasm.

"It's really a bit soon to talk about it."

"Bill won't go back there."

"I wouldn't be too sure; you know how perverse he is. In any case, we've got to prevent him going bankrupt. The house is in a terrible state. Once I've paid the debts, I'll have the roof looked at."

"I think you ought to try writing to him," urged his wife.

"I'll think that out; I've got to write him before long anyway. I should know about the farms by the end of the summer; Bolam's seeing the tenants with Bill's solicitor in two weeks' time." Simon yawned. "I think I'll go to bed; it's been a long day."

By the time the farms were sold and the creditors paid, there wasn't much over. Except for twenty acres round the house, all the land had gone.

Simon sat in the dining-room at Barmoor staring into the cold double grate. Through the tall windows behind him, the setting sun flooded the room. He turned to the outline in the glass of the Lammermuir Hills to the North. It was time to drive over to Lennel. The idea of staying alone at Barmoor sent shivers down his spine. Bill had told him once, that in that very room, a black object had hurtled at him. Ever since then, there'd been a small wooden cross on the mantlepiece. Simon got up and walked up and down. The wallpaper was starting to come away from one corner of the room. A tell-tale mark of damp showed on the ceiling. His worst fears had been confirmed earlier that day by the builders from Green-law: parts of the house had deep, dry rot.

"Any idea what it'll cost to put it right?" Simon had asked.

"It's difficult to say, Mr Sitwell. It's not just the roof, we'd have to seal off the whole North wing; that's where the damp you see in the dining-room is coming from."

"Can't you put any figure on it at all? I won't hold you to it; I just want some idea of how much money's involved. Perhaps ten thousand?" Simon asked, hopefully.

They shook their heads. "If you were to double that, you might be a bit closer, Mr Sitwell. It's a big job; aye, a big job."

Simon walked about now, realising that, his mother would have to come to the rescue, if the house were to be saved. £20,000 was too much. He'd paid less than half that for his house in Sussex. Was it worth it? he asked himself. If it were fixed, what next would happen? Simon began talking to himself: "If I had only this place and the policies consisting of the garden and the rest of the land, I'd live off the land, literally. The kitchen garden is enormous and in quite good order; I'd grow fruit in the greenhouses, exotics like peaches and melons, to be sold in Newcastle or Edinburgh. Then there were the lawns; they could be used as paddocks; I'd have a cow and a few pigs, chicken and geese, maybe a sheep or two; I'd never be hungry. If I put my mind to it, I could even make a living! Raise a few calves to help pay the rates."

Carried away, he looked out the window. In the deepening shadows, Brackenside, the best farm, was still just visible on the horizon. The view was the same, as before the war when he'd been a boy. As a child, he'd taken everything for granted. The land was the family's surely as far as the eye could see; he could walk over the fields to his heart's content; shoot rabbits, pick hazel-nuts, gather mushrooms, fish in the streams. He was "Master Simon", the old General's youngest son; it'd never entered his head that his rights and privileges would ever be questioned.

'I'd be trespassing now, I suppose,' he reflected bitterly as he stood there. 'The other side of that ha-ha belongs to Mr Reavley; technically, I'd be off-limits, if I walked over that field without first asking him.' Simon flung himself down in a chair, his body taut with frustration and anger. 'To think that one bloody fool could have let this happen.' This land, loved and taken care of by his forefathers. All gone! The house isolated on a tiny island of twenty acres; it was incredible. Twenty acres! Why, that was the same as he had surrounding his house in Sussex; the stockbroker belt.

Simon walked next door into the saloon; the last of the sun just caught the edge of the oval dome, thirty feet above. What a lovely room. Well, at least Bill wasn't bankrupt, he didn't owe anyone a penny; that in itself was something. But what about the house? It couldn't be left like this!

A few hours later, he had a drink with Betty. To have Lennel to return to at the end of the day was really marvellous, an oasis in the barren, hopeless situation he found himself, trespassing on his own history, as it were.

"But supposing he ever does come back? What on earth will he do?" Betty asked, curled up in her chair by the drawing-room fire.

Aslam, the Pakistani butler, came into the room to hold the door open for them, as they went in for dinner. All very pre-war, Simon thought. "Bill never did like the country," Betty continued. "He'd get bored within five minutes."

"I had a letter from him the other day," Simon said.

"Oh? How is he?"

"He's still at sea."

"I wrote and suggested that the family buy the place from him and do it up."

"What did he say?"

"He wrote to my mother: he wasn't prepared to sell it. It's academic anyway; it needs £20,000 to stop it from falling down."

Betty didn't seem to have heard him. "What he ought to have is his own ship." she said suddenly. "I came across Gordon Ellis when I was in Berwick the other day; didn't I tell you? He said that Bill could be running a trawler; he might keep it in Tweedmouth or somewhere like that."

"What else did he say?"

"You can get most of the cost of building it paid for; there's some sort of Government scheme. Why don't you talk to him?"

"I will." Gordon Ellis was a great friend of Simon's.

"If he could have something like a trawler, he'd be perfectly happy. He might even make a very good living; Gordon seemed to think they were all doing very well."

"Sounds quite an interesting idea," said Simon.

"I've got to go into Berwick tomorrow; why don't you come with me? We could go on up to Eyemouth and talk to people."

"I've got to go back to London, I'm afraid."

"Oh, surely it wouldn't matter if you stayed another day?"

Simon sighed. How could she be expected to understand what modern business life was like. "I'd love to, but I can't."

"D'you like what you're doing?"

"Yes, I do actually; but I get a bit tired sometimes."

"It's a pity you weren't the eldest son."

Simon didn't say anything. She had a point; at least he wasn't so damned pig-headed as his brother. "I don't suppose I'd have done any better," he said.

"But you're more of a country person; you'd have liked it here."

"I don't think I would."

"Why not? You're not a bad shot, and you're good with horses."

"Business is quite stimulating; I'm involved with so many other people; their families, their hopes, and ambitions."

"What d'you mean?"

"If your business does well, it affects everyone associated with you. If you give a chap a raise, he's able to buy his wife a nice dress or take his family for a holiday abroad. That sort of situation does not arise if you're running an estate."

"I wish I'd been a businessman," said Betty.

She'd finished her soup before Simon had even started and was now lighting a cigarette.

"You'd have been very good," agreed Simon. "I can't see anything difficult about it, which is easy to say after you've done it."

"Well, I started the knitting factory; it's doing jolly well. Lennel Knitwear; they send stuff all over the world."

That's true, thought Simon.

"What we ought to do is start a trawler company for Bill."

What an extraordinary person, thought Simon as he drank his soup. Dumped by Bill, and here she is thinking of ways to get him going again; bloody marvellous, isn't it! But he held his tongue.

"Why can't you stay here till Monday? Surely you can tell the office you've been delayed?" Betty was determined to pursue the trawler idea.

"I can't."

"Why on earth not?"

Sitting there with the candles burning, Aslam hovering with the food, the dogs in a heap in front of the fire, it was difficult not to weaken. If only he could give up the rat race; how nice to be able to live like this. He ate a mouthful of pheasant; Aslam approached and filled his wine-glass. This was the way to live; the blood of his wayward ancestors still filled his veins. How nice never to have to go to London again; to have to catch that awful 7.59 from Horsham; to wait at Three Bridges for the connection to London Bridge; and then the draughty walk across the river to the City. How trivial the office seemed to him, sitting in this lovely room with it's polished furniture and the silver, the firelight, and the disorderly luxurious atmosphere.

"There'll be three extra for luncheon tomorrow, Aslam. You'd better warn Mrs Fairbairn," said Betty. deep in thought until then.

"Very well, Madam."

"Who's coming?" asked Simon .

"Tony and Tish Barber and Susan Askew. They'd love to see you; they're always asking after you."

"I'm not sure I'll be here."

"Why can't you be here then?"

"There's a chap coming up from Morpeth to see me."

"What d'you mean? You said you paid off all the creditors."

"I have."

"Well, who's this chap?"

"I haven't met him but I believe he's the Liberal candidate for Berwick at the next election."

"You're not going into politics, surely?"

"No, of course not."

"What are you doing meeting him then? You'd far better stay and have lunch here."

"I've an idea he's interested in renting Barmoor. I should see him," said Simon.

"Yes, perhaps you'd better; you didn't tell me this."

"I put an advertisement in *The Times*," said Simon, guiltily.

"We'll have coffee in the drawing-room, Aslam." Betty got up; she took Simon's arm. "Come on, you silly old thing," she said affectionately. "There's a good play on the telly tonight."

ANOTHER YEAR went by. Simon's visits to the North became less frequent; with all the business concluded and the creditors paid, there was just the house to see to. Raising of the money for the builders had been less of a problem than he'd imagined. Simon had shown his mother the builders' report and their estimate for doing the work. "If we can get the house repaired, there's a good chance I can let it," he had told her. "It's ideally situated and the rent suggested will pay the rates and leave quite a bit for maintenance.

"Are you sure all this has to be done, darling?" His mother put down the sheets of paper and looked at him. "You couldn't help, I suppose?" she asked.

He shook his head. He'd already laid out more than he could afford; in another year his daughter would be in boarding school. "I'm paying for Bill's son's education as it is," Simon said.

Conty Sitwell stared at the window; how she loved Victoria Square, people always coming and going and dropping in. Her mind wandered; her thoughts were a long way from Barmoor.

"Well, there are my mother's pearls; I believe they're rather valuable, and that tiara, I can't remember when I last wore it," she was almost talking to herself.

"You've got some valuable paintings too, you know."

"D'you think so?"

"Those Hitchens, Mama. And you've got two Epsteins."

"But I'm leaving everything in the house to you, darling."

Simon shrugged his shoulders. "Yes, I know."

"And I'm dividing my jewellery between Ann and your girl."

"It's more important to save the house; there's no alternative," Simon said, wondering what was in his mother's head: she didn't seem very concerned. Quite calm and resigned actually; some women would've been in tears. Perhaps she's feeling some of the tragedy is her fault. Strange, the way she's never uttered a word of criticism against Bill. Odd too, her attitude to money; she still only gave him a pound for his birthday and Christmas; almost miserly, certainly very tight indeed; yet here she was, so relaxed, willing to fork out £20,000. What an enigma! he thought, but her voice sounded weary. "Alright, darling," she said. "I'll see what else there is for you to sell, but you must tell Ann, though she won't mind; I've given her quite a lot already. I expect she's lost most of it by now."

She smiled and Simon laughed. "It's very good of you, Mama, to help like this. When did you last hear from Bill?"

"I had a letter a fortnight ago, posted from Singapore."

"He's still on the *Chris*, is he?"

"Yes; I must say it doesn't sound much fun."

Simon could imagine what it was like; a Honduran-registered Liberty ship crewed by the sweepings of the Bowery. For Bill to be second mate of an old tramp like that after having his own corvette in the war; he certainly had come down with a thump. Simon felt momentarily sorry for his brother.

He sat there quietly, thinking to himself. The sensible thing to do must be to let the house even though Bill might return one day. Betty was still enthusiastic about the trawler idea; it had decent possibilities; at least it'd give his brother something and the house would be lived in; but Bill was so unpredictable and perverse. Then there was Phoebette's scheme; buy the place for the children and set up a trust. But one thing at a time. First, the repair money had to be raised; then the builders given the go-ahead.

"**Alright, Mr Sitwell**," said the embryo Member for Berwick-on-Tweed. "That seems reasonable enough; shall we put our solicitors in touch with each other? They can draw up the lease."

"Fine," said Simon. "Don't do anything for a week, though. I must cable my brother and have his permission; I think this ought to have his blessing. I'll send him a radiogram tomorrow."

The reply was not long in forthcoming.

"Letting out of the question. Letter follows."

The letter arrived a week later, Bill made it clear, he proposed cancelling the Power of Attorney.

"I'm sorry about this," Simon said into the telephone to the anxious tenant. "My brother is a bit difficult at times."

"Let me know if he changes his mind."

'I wish everyone was a reasonable as you are,' Simon thought.

'Where do we go from here?' he asked himself. The alternative idea of selling the place to Ann and himself also fell on stony soil.

"It's absolutely out of the question," Bill wrote to his mother. "I might live there myself one day, even if I don't intend to yet."

'Fair enough,' thought Simon. But when would he? If left empty for any length of time, the house would deteriorate again. Leaning back in his chair, he looked round his office. "If I gave as much thought to the firm's business as I do on Bill's, I'd be a tycoon by now," he reflected. A knock on the door interrupted: his secretary bringing him coffee.

"You asked to be reminded to telephone Mr Recksten today," she said.

"Thanks, Ruth. Good job you remembered; I wouldn't have. Please ask Mr Martens to see me."

His friend and associate came into the room.

"Hullo, Peter. What're we doing about the Recksten renewal?"

It was time to get on with immediate business.

Joan Castle before
she met Bill

Joan Castle Sitwell,
actress, painted
publicity photo

PAYING GUESTS

IN RIO DE JANEIRO on a February Sunday, Simon stretched out on the Copacabana beach, eating an orange. Luxury hotels nearby overshadowed the busy road; he'd checked in four days previously but this was the first chance he had, early in the morning, to lay down with the sea. It seemed like a dream come true; to be sent to Brazil in the middle of the English winter. He'd jumped at the chance, when it was suggested, of a meeting with the managers of the Brazilian government's tanker fleet.

It'd been a tough trip so far though; after working all day, the Brazilians took Simon to the many clubs to continue the talks. He didn't get back to his hotel before midnight, or later, yet at eight the following morning, there'd be a car outside waiting to take him to the first meeting that day.

Even today, he only had the morning to himself. He was being collected and taken out to lunch by an agent; doubtless there'd be the usual sightseeing trip also, then back to his host's house for cocktails and supper. It's the same wherever you go, thought Simon wearily. He'd been on the receiving end so often, he'd forgotten how many times a peaceful Sunday had been interrupted by an unplanned business commitment. He walked down to the water's edge. He needed to be left alone longer, to recover from the week.

Then he remembered the telephone call from Friday evening. He hadn't been there to take it but the reception desk had handed him a slip with his key at 2 A.M. It was no effort to put the call aside, after the party at the Yacht Club; he'd gone straight from the office, with no time for a quick shower and change.

"Do best phone Monday. Ruth." Short, to the point, his secretary didn't waste words.

All weekend he wondered what might have happened; it was unlike her to worry him unless it was important.

Monday he was able to get through to London.

"Your sister rang; she wanted to get hold of you urgently," said the secretary. "It's about your brother."

I might have known, thought Simon. "Go on," he said.

"It's about his son; Ann says they can't keep him in school any longer. She wondered, as you were in Rio, whether you might go to New York on the way back and talk to Bill."

"Holy Moses!"

"It's not a very good line," said Simon, groaning inwardly and trying to gain a little time. "Did she give you an address?"

"She said you had it; care of someone called Castle, I believe. Joan Castle, that's it!"

The actress? Bloody appropriate, thought Simon. "Okay, Ruth. Tell Ann I received her message; I'll see what I can do."

The last thing he wanted was to see his brother; and he had to admit, he longed to get home. A business trip in itself had no glamour; offices were much the same wherever he went. Simon had looked forward to having a before-breakfast swim each day while he was in Rio; the sea was only a few hundred yards from his hotel window. But he'd needed all the sleep he could get for the early morning meetings.

He found it difficult to make up his mind about New York. It'd be cheaper certainly to go there on the way home rather then make a special journey from London later; and something had to be done about Bill's son, but the Power of Attorney episode annoyed Simon, over the way Bill had stopped him from letting Barmoor. It still stood empty; the rates and other bills needed to be paid. Simon didn't look forward to asking his mother for more money.

"I'd better go, I suppose," he said to himself; an extra day away from the office won't matter.

The journey took 24 hours; with a delay at Caracas. The airport at New York was closed by fog; so the big jet put down at midnight, at the half-completed Dulles airfield near Washington; the final leg of the journey was by bus; it was breakfast time when he checked in to his hotel. After a short rest, Simon made his way to an address that turned out to be an apartment block uptown.

A smartly-dressed woman opened the door. "You must be Simon!" she exclaimed, obviously very taken aback.

"I'm looking for Bill."

"He's not here, he's at work."

"How can I get a message to him?"

"He'll probably call me during his lunch break."

"Could you ask him to telephone me at the Gladstone? Tell him I'm only there tonight; I leave for London in the morning."

"Of course I will. darling. I'm so pleased to have met you."

Actresses! They all talked like that. Simon left.

Shivering in his thin tropical suit, he returned to the hotel and waited. He must've dozed off; when the telephone rang he didn't remember where he was at first.

"It's Bill," said the voice at the other end.

They talked for a few minutes.

"Okay, I'll see you tonight; seven o'clock in the hotel bar."

As his brother walked into the Gladstone, Simon thought, 'I wonder why he always has his hair cut so short; it doesn't suit him.'

Bill seemed pleased to see Simon. "How's everyone at home?"

Bit by bit, Simon learnt that Bill was working in a warehouse somewhere downtown. We'll have a drink before business, Simon thought. It'd loosen tongues; he also felt half-dead with fatigue after the journey from Rio.

"By the way, I asked Joan to join us," Bill said casually, as the actress walked through the door.

Simon couldn't believe it! All this way to talk to him and he has to bring an actress along. Simon ordered her a drink; perhaps she'll push off in half-an-hour; he thought. She'd better!

But it was not to be; an hour passed and she showed no sign of leaving. Simon looked at his watch, deliberately avoiding looking at her. "We'd better go get something to eat, Bill."

"That's a swell idea," she said. "Where shall we go?"

Simon felt ready to explode.

"I know," she exclaimed triumphantly. "The 21 Club; they do the best steaks in town."

Simon shuddered and wondered how much money he had left; it was quite obvious who'd have to pay the bill. He said nothing and glanced at his brother; Bill sat on his bar stool staring into space. Simon'd get no help from that quarter. "This is just so ridiculous," he muttered to himself.

Famous as she was, though in the past, the actress was fawned upon in the restaurant; Bill and Simon sat silently as Joan discussed the menu with the head waiter.

"I'll just have an omelette," said Bill, "I'm not very hungry."

Bill sat next to Joan, looking bloody miserable. Not a surprise, thought Simon.

Simon took a mouthful of food, then laid down his fork. "I'm sorry, Joan; but I've got to talk to Bill. There are family problems."

"Of course you have to, darling; don't bother about me." She put her arm on Bill's shoulder. "I know all about the difficulties Bill's having; you just talk as much as you like, darling." She gave Simon a glittering smile.

Simon looked at his brother, thinking 'Come on, say something'. But Bill avoided him, staring at his plate. After a longer silence, Simon thought, it's now or never. "Alright," he started. "We'd best talk about Michael first."

For the next five minutes Simon talked about Bill's son and the schooling problems. There was very little conversation.

"I'll write to you about it," said his brother. "We can't discuss it now; I'll have to think over what you told me and let you know."

"When d'you think that'll be?"

"I don't know." Bill paused. "I just don't know."

"We can't let it drift; he's got to be educated," insisted Simon.

Bill shook his head. "I'll let you know," he repeated.

Joan glared at Simon from across the table. "I believe you've come here just to upset him," she hissed.

"What?"

"Your family. All you want to do is upset him; I know all about it. You just want to make his life a misery. You don't know what he's going through; you should try working the hours he does."

She patted his arm. Simon shook his head in disbelief.

"Say something, Bill," he pleaded. "Tell her that I'm paying for your son's education."

Bill hung his head. "That's true," he muttered.

"And what's so wonderful about that?" said Joan. " What d'you think families are for?"

A flood of weariness descended over Simon; he pushed his plate away. All those miles for this treatment! He looked at his watch; just 24 hours earlier, the DC8 airliner was circling Idlewilde airport trying to land in the fog. A young man, shot in the neck and paralysed by a stray bullet at a football match, lay on a stretcher in the aisle. Put on board at Caracas, he moaned loudly. Simon found a sponge in his overnight bag, for the nurse and stewardess to wipe the man's forehead. An argument with the cabin crew ensued. The nurse sent messages to the captain: if the plane wasn't landed at New York, where an ambulance waited to rush the man to the Mark Hopkins, he'd die. Simon heard the flaps lowered, then the noise of the gear going down. His sympathies were up front in the cockpit; he imagined the pilot doing an instrument approach, the diminishing altitude being read out to him as he looked for the runway. Then came the familiar roar; the crew decided on an overshoot, to land elsewhere. Poor devils, Simon thought: facing a situation like that at the end of the long flight from Venezuela.

Simon pulled himself together; for the umpteenth time that evening he asked himself why his brother wanted Joan along.

"Let's change the subject, shall we?" he said.

"That's right, darling. Let's talk about something else."

Joan fluttered her eyelashes at him over the table.

God, you are awful, thought Simon. As for Bill, he was just too scared to open his mouth. "I'm afraid we must talk about Barmoor," Simon spoke again, almost apologetically.

Joan leaned forward, all smiles. "Yes, let's talk about Barmoor," she said.

Simon paused, wondering how to phrase the next bit more diplomatically. "Could you tell me what your plans are?"

"There you go again, I knew it! You came here to upset us. Well, get this straight, Mister; I ain't letting you." She gave his brother a hug. No wonder she no longer had real parts, Simon thought.

"I know you've cancelled the Power of Attorney," Simon went on hurriedly, ignoring her. "But the house just can't be left empty."

"Watch it!" said Joan aggressively.

Is this really happening? Simon thought wildly. He wanted to yell at the woman: Much more of this, I'll walk out and you can pay the damned bill! He felt himself flushing.

"Waiter. Can you fill our glasses, please?" He needed a minute to collect his thoughts; what was the best way to deal with this unprovoked onslaught? Bill must've said quite nasty things to her about the family.

"Bill," Simon began. "You know very well I haven't come all this way just to criticise you."

"That's right, Joan," Bill murmured. "He's only doing his best."

The actress turned on him. "Doing his best? Why shouldn't he be doing his best? Your family just sat around while you tried to keep the home going; they've never lifted a finger to help you. Why, you've slaved away all your life trying to keep Barmoor. Now, he comes here; he just wants to give you more worries and problems. Well, I'm not letting him."

She took a drink from her glass. 'That swig of claret probably set me back a couple of dollars,' said Simon to himself. Ridiculous; what did this woman sitting opposite him know about the past, about Barmoor, the quarry, or indeed anything?

"I'm sorry if I'm annoying you, Joan. If you like, we'll finish our meal and I'll talk to Bill later," Simon said diplomatically.

"I'm not letting you!"

Simon half stood up; he felt himself shaking with anger. "Have it your own way, then. I'm going to ask Bill a few questions and I'd be obliged if you didn't interfere."

They glared at each other. His brother sat fiddling with a roll of bread on his sideplate.

"What I want to know; what everyone wants to know," Simon said, speaking directly to his brother, "is what are your plans?"

Bill sat silently, his eyes focussed on a corner of the ceiling above them. Joan opened her mouth to say something; Simon held up his hand. "Just a moment, Joan."

She looked at Bill. "He's too tired, the poor darling. Do you know what time he leaves the apartment?"

Simon shook his head. "I just want to know what his plans are."

"I'll tell you what our plans are," she said fiercely.

Our plans, what's she mean? thought Simon. Are we playing at Alice in Wonderland?

"We're going to live at Barmoor; that's what'll happen." She paused to gather up her strength for the next outburst: "Everybody knows what you want, Mister Simon. You just want your brother's house."

Simon put his hands over his face. She must be round the bloody bend. The time for politeness was passed. What's more, it was late and he had an early flight to catch in the morning. "Will you tell her to shut up, Bill?"

His brother sat there quietly, as if he'd lost all ability to say anything.

"You're mad," said Simon bluntly to Joan.

"Not as mad as you think; I know your little game. You've always been jealous of your brother; you just want to get your hands on Barmoor."

"I see," he said wearily. " So you're going to live there, are you?"

"Yes, we are; aren't we, darling?" She kissed Bill on the cheek.

"I wish you luck." Simon went on, sarcastically. "I know it's none of my business, but could I just ask what you intend to do there? There are no farms left and only a small plot round the house."

"We're going to have people to stay; they'll be glad to pay us."

Simon burst out laughing. "I see. Have you ever been there?"

"No, I haven't; but Bill's told me all about it."

"Really?" He gave his brother a look but Bill was determined not to catch his eye; he sat there stoney-faced, examining his nails.

"You'll see," said Joan. "We'll have people queueing up to stay."

"You'll need to spend some money on it first; it could do with new mattresses and extra bathrooms."

"It's got nothing to do with you anymore. Why d'you think we stopped the Power of Attorney? You're not as smart as you think."

Simon stood up fully.

"You can stay here if you like but I'm going back to my hotel; I'll take care of the bill on my way out."

Suddenly, Joan got up and came towards him. Putting her arms round him, she kissed him on the cheek. "I think you're darling."

Simon shrugged her off and left.

How curious, how absurd, Simon thought: she got her big break as a stand-in, in *Sailor Beware*, but that was a comedy. Bill's life wasn't, except perhaps to her. At least, she was making it one.

A bell-boy interrupted Simon's thinking, as he was signing his travellers cheques at the hotel's accounts desk. "There's a call for you, sir; would you care to take it here?"

The voice at the other end was very faint.

"Speak up; I can't hear you."

"It's Bill. I'm sorry about Joan."

Standing there in the crowded lobby, Simon felt a sudden surge of pain and love for his wretched brother.

"That's alright."

"She's not as bad as you think."

Simon was silent; a plan took shape in his head. "Bill, are you there? Where are you? Good. Stay where you are; I'll pick you up in five minutes."

"What d'you mean?"

"I'm on my way to the airport; I'll pick you up and you can come home with me."

"That's very good of you, Simon. I can't. You don't understand."

"For Christ's sake, Bill. Leave while you can; I've got tickets and enough money. I'll pick you up in five minutes, okay?"

"I can't."

"Bill, please!"

"I can't. You don't understand."

Simon understood only too well; his brother's brains, if he had any left, had gone down with his trousers, to reveal nothing there either.

The lift attendant caught Simon's eye. "Your taxi's here, sir." He hovered nearby; Simon nodded his thanks.

"Bill, that woman's not good for you; for God's sake leave her. Come back to England with me; I've got a trawler lined up for you, for you to captain and profit by."

"It's very good of you, Simon; but I can't. Thanks for the dinner."

Simon opened his mouth to try again but there was a click; the line was dead. He walked to the entrance of the hotel pausing to distribute five dollar bills to the assembled staff. "I nearly did it," he said to himself. "Very nearly."

Another year passed before Bill and Joan came to England. Simon had been to Barmoor once or twice to see that everything was alright and that somehow the bills were paid. But the boy's education remained a problem; Ann had a letter from Bill but, as expected, it didn't say much.

The dinner incident in New York still infuriated Simon, yet his feelings of pity for Bill were stronger. When asked by his mother how he got on with his brother, he shrugged. "I don't hit it off with actresses; born under their own stars, I suppose."

"I'm told Joan's got lots of money and plans to do up Barmoor," his mother said.

"A sable coat from an ex-husband doesn't make her rich."

His remark exasperated his mother. "Well, I think she's very nice, so there," she said emphatically. "They'll have paying guests; I think that's rather a good idea."

"I wish them luck; if the weather's fine and they don't over-charge, they might do well."

"I wonder what his guests will pay?" mused his mother. "But I suppose Bill can go over to Fenton and see Tony; there's always Bamburgh for comparison."

"Perhaps. He'll have to get himself a car to get there; the one I gave him is just a run-about," said Simon.

"I didn't know you'd given Bill a car."

"Just a small Renault." Left standing in the stable yard. Bill must've fled in haste, abandoning the car, empty bottles and dirty dishes everywhere. He'd gone to pieces certainly. "Who'll cook for the visitors?" Simon asked.

"Oh, I expect he'll find someone qualified."

Simon still believed in the trawler idea; he and Betty formed a Company with Gordon Ellis as a shareholder; a friend of his at Lloyd's, Andrew Berry, had also put up money. After seeing the White Fish Authority at Granton, a little port near Edinburgh, Simon went to Eyemouth to discuss the Government's grant scheme with the builders and interviewed a possible skipper. If the scheme went through, they, Border Trawlers Limited, would get an outright grant plus a loan at very low interest rates. But Bill clearly wouldn't be part of this, till he failed again at Barmoor.

Joan too would have to fail him, but then Bill had put all those strange notions into her head. It was a horrifying thought that his brother felt so badly about the family, and even worse about Simon. What'd happened to give Bill cause? Simon had always been as helpful as he could; modest, indeed almost subservient in all their conversations. Did Bill really think such bad things about him?

Simon sighed. He found himself wondering when it had started and whether he could've done anything to have prevented it.

It must be jealousy, perhaps even a deep-seated resentment, Simon decided. But why? Bill wasn't pleased at Simon going off to the war before him, but it was only a matter of months and hadn't been his fault. R.N.V.R officers weren't called up until later. Then there was the Distinguished Flying Cross; that hadn't been Simon's idea either! He'd made a point of telling people it'd simply "come with the rations". But Bill too was mentioned in dispatches and received a commendation for rescuing a drowning sailor.

All the same, he must have told Joan some quite awful stories for her to attack him the way she did. Help somebody and they kick you in the teeth, Simon thought bitterly. Any friend he'd ever lent money to had in turn destroyed the friendship.

"Didn't you hear what I said, darling?" His mother asked.

"Sorry, Mama; I was miles away."

"I said, will the children be going to Barmoor this summer?"

"I shouldn't think so."

"Why not? They all seem to love it so much."

Simon hesitated to answer. Ann had written to Joan asking if they could come up during summer holidays but had been told it'd cost £30 a day per head; Ann and Phoebette were furious.

"Joan wanted to charge us the same as the p.g's," Simon said.

"Are you sure you're right, darling?"

Simon got up. "It doesn't matter, Mama."

His mother looked at him expectantly.

"If I don't go now, I'll miss the 6.18," he said.

Joan's paying guest venture lasted two summers; there wasn't enough for guests to do and they didn't get value for their money. It wasn't long before another crisis loomed.

"I've had to send Bill a little money," his mother announced on one of Simon's visits. "He seems to be feeling very poor; not many Americans are coming over this summer."

"Well, let me know when he's next in London," Simon said.

When finally they met again, Simon told Bill, "I've made rather a fool of myself. I've set up a company to purchase a trawler and I'm just realising that I haven't got the time or experience to run it."

"What sort of trawler?"

"Not a very large one; about 80 feet overall."

"What made you do that?"

Simon wanted to say that it was to keep his brother at Barmoor. "The projections made it seem a good idea. The government will subsidise the building costs and you get the tax benefits."

Bill grunted in his customary way.

"It's the sort of thing that might interest you, actually," Simon went on hopefully. "The company will operate out of Eyemouth. I've got a very good skipper; he'd own the nets and gear. Trouble is, I've no one to run it; you know, take care of the business side."

Bill shook his head. "It's very good of you to think of me, Simon, but I don't think you quite understand. I can ship out tomorrow as master of an Esso tanker at £10,000 a year."

"£10,000 a year? That's a hell of a lot!"

"I can get a job any time I choose," said Bill confidently.

The man's mad, thought Simon, but I can't very well call him a liar to his face. I know damn well he hasn't got his master's ticket; he's dreaming in one of Joan's fading dramas.

By 1971, Bill's marriage to Joan was running on the rocks. To earn a living, he'd gone back to sea; not as master of a large tanker but as a deck officer on a ship heading to China to be broken up. Simon saw him on his return, passing through London on his way back to Barmoor where Joan was still living.

It was quite like the old days, hearing about the long trip from

Hamburg to Shanghai. Bill's wallet was bulging with notes.

"I made them pay me in cash," he announced.

"I wouldn't carry all that around; why not put it in the bank?"

"No, I'm going to hand it over to Joan; as you know, I'm not very good with money. She says I owe her thousands of pounds."

"What? Why?"

"It's the money she spent doing up the house."

"But she can't have spent that much, surely?"

"She says she did. Matter of fact, I've given her all the furniture in the green drawing-room."

"What?" Simon gasped; he couldn't believe his ears, as he knew Bill and Joan were fighting like cat and dog.

Bill repeated himself, speaking slowly and deliberately.

"But it's absolutely priceless!" Simon said. "The best furniture in the house; don't you realize, it's all matching Louis XV; worth a fortune! I don't understand."

"Tough luck, then," replied his brother icily.

"D'you realize what you've done? There's huge money there."

"What's money!"

"I give up," said Simon. "The furniture could've paid for all the house repairs and more besides."

"Don't worry; she's not going to run off with it."

"But it's hers, isn't it? Has she given you a receipt or anything?"

"She tore up the mortgage document."

"Mortgage document; what mortgage document?"

"I'd an agreement drawn up, to keep her quiet."

"What did it say?"

"That I owed her all sorts of money."

"How much?"

"Mind your own business."

Simon felt near to tears; what a waste of time it'd all been. "Is there no way you can get it back?"

"No, there isn't. Now, if you don't mind, we'll talk about something else."

Just like my mother, thought Simon. "How long are you back for this time?" he asked.

"Depends really; there might be a job for me out in Canada."

"Why don't you stay here and run Border Trawlers?"

"For the very good reason that, if I'm under the same roof as Joan for more than a week or two, I'd go borderland mad."

"I didn't know it was as bad as that."

"Well, it is."

"I never liked her; remember New York?" Asking his brother why he didn't defend him was a temptation, but it was pointless to open old wounds. "What's the trouble? She get on your nerves?"

"She goes on at me; always nagging. I never get peace or quiet; I'm pretty tired, I can tell you."

Simon nodded. He felt sorry for Bill, more than he wanted to. "Anything I can do to help?"

Bill shook his head. "Thanks, I'll just have to put up with it."

"Does she want to go on living in the house?" Simon asked.

"Yes, I think so. People are very good to her, you know. Trouble is, she can't drive a car; if she's asked out to a meal, someone has to collect her and then take her back."

"I see. I wouldn't care to live there by myself either," said Simon.

Bill smiled. "Too bloody true; I told you about that dark scary thing in the dining-room, didn't I?"

"Yes, long time ago. But what happened to the white lady?"

"She was supposedly shot by a silver bullet in the last century."

"Nobody's ever seen her?"

"No, I don't think so."

They both sat silently thinking about their old home and it's ghosts. "The place I never liked was the wood up at Watchlaw," said Bill. "That's where Ann heard the hounds giving tongue for no clear reason one summer afternoon."

"Yes; and it's on that bit of the Ford road that someone was chased by a bale of hay."

They both shuddered.

"I'd have run for my life too," said Simon.

Bill nodded. "Much worse than seeing a ghost! Fancy walking down the road on a summer's afternoon without a breath of wind and suddenly a bale's blowing down the road at you!"

They were both quiet then; each remembering the days before the war when they'd been boys and went with the bogie carts to lead the pikes of hay from the fields.

Bill sighed and stood up. "I better be off to catch my train."

"Let me know how you get on," said Simon.

They shook hands and parted.

Several years passed. Bill settled into a regular job with a Canadian company based in New Brunswick and was master of a ship running out of Saint John. He appeared back on leave from time to time and usually went to Barmoor where Joan lived happily.

Simon saw them together when they stayed with his mother at Victoria Square. He still disliked Joan but gave her credit for living at Barmoor alone; she seemed to love the place and was forever going round with little pots of paint and rearranging things.

A new drama was only a question of time, however. While Joan and Bill were in London, a thief broke in and took all the silver.

"Simon! I've been trying to get hold of you all day." It was Ann screaming down the telephone. There was a burglary at Barmoor; the silver's gone."

He'd expected this and still had insurance. "Anything else?"

"I don't know, the police are still there."

"Wasn't anyone in the house?"

"I don't know." There was a pause. "I thought we'd put it in the bank," said Ann.

"We did; but Bill and Joan took it all out, when he revoked the Power of Attorney; don't you remember? Anyway, thank God, the silver's insured," sighed Simon.

"Did you do that?"

"Yes. When Bill went off in the *Cairngowan*."

"That's years ago. It's still covered?" Ann asked anxiously.

"Yes, I've been paying the premiums; the policy is in my desk."

"I spoke to Joan," Ann said. "She was almost hysterical; they were her icons."

Simon felt himself colouring. "To hell with her bloody beliefs. What about other family stuff; the lovely georgian teapot and the knives and forks with our coat-of-arms?"

Having all the best furniture handed over in lieu of so-called debt was bad enough; now the silver had been nicked too. Simon recalled that he'd noticed on one of his rare visits to his old home, how all the silver had been laid out, in display, on a table in the oval drawing-room.

"Hopeless, absolutely," he muttered. One thing, then another; he wished the whole place to burn down.

Later, he phoned Joan. *The Yorkshire Post* had interviewed her.

"You shouldn't have talked to the press," Simon said.

"But my icons; they're priceless," she moaned.

"Did the reporter ask about the worth? What'd you tell them?"

"I offered a reward."

"How much?"

"Two thousand pounds."

"Meaning they're worth twenty thousand pounds, then?"

"At least that, darling."

"But the silver at Barmoor is only insured for ten thousand."

"I just want my icons back."

Simon almost put the receiver back on the hook. The silly idiot. If the underwriters got to hear this, they'd apply average and Bill would get next-to-nothing. Simon fumed as he paced up and down his office. How absolutely in character for her; anything for a quick buck! Like the so-called mortgage on the furniture; now she'd scoop up all the insurance money! Anger and frustration welled up again; why'd such appalling people come into his life?

It's the same for everybody, he reminded himself, as he searched for the insurance document; he really mustn't blow his top like this. Turn back the rug a bit; heaven knows what you'll find. All families have problems; delinquent children, parents fighting incessantly, a sister-in-law who shop-lifts.

The door of his office opened; it was Ruth, his secretary.

"Where did we file the Barmoor policy?" he asked.

"I'll find it. And, the travel people want to know whether you'll be going on to Vancouver from Seattle, or coming straight back?"

"Let me check my schedule."

The girl bent over the filing cabinet looking for the policy.

Simon tried to concentrate on his forthcoming business trip; it was too full a schedule. "Exporting is fun," Harold Macmillan had said. What idiocy! All those early morning checkouts; the hanging around in airports; the late nights and chronic sense of not having enough sleep; the endless effort of dictating the day's events into the tape-recorder before switching off the light. Yes, great fun!

"Here it is." Ruth held up the policy.

"Ring them up and put them on notice, would you please? And ask them to send round a claim form while you're about it."

"What's happened?" asked the girl.

"What hasn't happened, you mean." Simon put his head in his hands. Was he doomed to bow under the problems of Barmoor; on his back for evermore?

Ruth looked at him expectantly.

"The place was broken into and all the silver taken."

She shook her head. Simon sat back in his chair. "I thought this might happen; I'm just wondering what's the next disaster. You'd better find the fire policy and make sure it's not about to lapse. That's all we need; the place a heap of ashes and no insurance."

The girl smiled. "I'll have a look for it; shouldn't take too long."

In due course, the claim was paid. Bill's visits to Barmoor became fewer, the intervals longer; no one was surprised when Joan's publicist announced she'd be divorcing "legendary sea captain," Bill Sitwell, but keeping his historic name and a bountiful share of his inheritance; yes, she'll have a cat named Sacheverell next.

"I wonder what she may do for an encore?" said Conty when Simon called on her.

"Grab all the lolly and scarper!"

"I do wish you wouldn't use such dreadful working-class expressions, darling."

"Sorry, Mama."

"It's all very tiresome, isn't it?"

Simon laughed. "That's rather understating things, isn't it?"

"I think it's probably quite a good thing." As usual, his mother was determined to see the bright side.

"Personally, I don't care a damn at this point what happens to either of them; I'm just concerned for the house." Simon at 55 years old was bad-tempered now, trying to cope with middle-age and business problems.

"Well, anyway; you're alright, aren't you, darling?"

Simon reflected for a minute before answering. "Yes, I suppose so. Considering I had no one to help me in the City, no relations or anything, I have done quite well; if that's what you mean."

"Deedle would have been as proud of you as I am," she said.

"A lot of it was luck. The £3000 of Uncle Gar's got me started. I'm not saying I haven't worked hard, I have; but I'm nowhere near the top of the tree and never will be. Another five years and I'll be retired; I've gotten as far as I ever will."

"Someone told me he'd seen Bill in London a week ago," said his mother, looking out the window at the pigeons in the square.

"I didn't know he'd been over. What was he doing?"

"Walking along arm-in-arm with a new woman."

He's got himself shacked up again, thought Simon.

"I'm glad he's found himself a young lady."

Conty spoke with feeling, as Simon sat silently. What a mess it all was! Joan would sue, take all the best furniture and leave. The house would be empty again, unless Bill returned to it.

"I wonder if she's got money," he said, thinking aloud. "Unless I'm completely wrong, this latest episode will ruin Bill for good."

"D'you realize it's almost twenty years since you and I went up to Middlesbrough to see him on the *Cairngowan*? You were quite wonderful, darling."

Simon looked at his mother; she was an old woman now and had to sit in her chair most of the time. No longer could she go to see her psychical associates at the L.S.A in Queensberry Place; but she seemed happy enough. A stream of friends, young and old, came to see her. "You mustn't mind when I die, darling," she said. It was as if she'd read his thoughts.

Simon felt a lump in his throat; he went over and kissed her.

"You're not going to die yet, Mama," he said cheerfully.

But he was to be proved wrong. A few days later, a caller found her dead in her armchair by the window.

ECLIPSE

AFTER MANY MONTHS of bitter wrangling, Bill's third divorce went through. Joan walked away from the Court a rich woman; the fact that he lived in a castle, and that his new wife-to-be was Joan's best friend, hadn't helped his case much. It didn't matter that Bill only had a few hundred dollars in his bank account; his appeal fell on deaf ears, he still had plenty of assets he could dispose of.

Simon was soon summoned to a flat in Kensington; it belonged to the new woman in Bill's life, Mary. Simon found her pleasant enough. What irritated him was the concern his brother appeared to show for one of her sons while not bothering about his own, who now was living in Copenhagen with Anna, the mother. For all her faults, Joan had been very good about Michael and often had him to stay at Barmoor.

Not surprisingly, Bill and Mary looked very despondent. "We'll have to sell the rest of the furniture," he told Simon.

Simon nodded, knowing the battle was lost. If only Bill had picked some rich widow. That might, just, have saved Barmoor.

Simon felt no anger or bitterness towards his brother now; just pity. It wasn't his fault he was weak and hopeless; he had inherited it somehow. He completely lacked any sense of responsibility and his apparent lack of concern for the history of his home, for all the lovely things in it, was appalling. With dismay, Simon remembered Bill's flippant remark, "What's money?"

Simon felt resigned. Having a row with his brother now would be pointless; nothing would change; the prelude, the last act was nearing quickly.

"You're welcome to anything you want," said Bill. "I'm having it all valued."

"I'll pay you for what I take," Simon said. He didn't expect or want any favours.

"You'd better go up and have a look round; I'll write to the lawyers and tell them to expect to hear from you."

"How will I get in?"

"Joan's still there."

"She'll let me in, will she?"

"I'll get the lawyers to write to her."

"What are your plans?" Simon asked.

"I'm flying back to Canada tomorrow. I've still got over a year to go before I'm pensioned off."

Thank God he's collecting a pension, thought Simon. At least it's something; he'd forgotten his brother had been with the same company for so long.

"What'll you do then?"

Bill pulled a face. "I don't know."

At least he didn't tell me to mind my own business, reflected Simon. This last setback must have chastened Bill considerably. His hair had gone white; but at least was longer than usual. Simon wondered if, at last, there'd be some words of regret or remorse; perhaps even a word of thanks for the help he'd tried to give him.

His brother noticed Simon looking at him expectantly; he stared back defiantly, I really do believe he hates my guts, thought Simon, as he walked down the stairs and out into the street.

"Have you been up there yet?" Simon recognised Mary's voice at the other end of the telephone.

"Not yet."

"I thought you said you were going up last weekend."

"I was, but it didn't suit Joan."

"Did you know we are appealing against the settlement?"

"Yes, you did say something about it."

"So, she wouldn't see you?" Mary continued.

"She was in Edinburgh last Saturday; I'll go up another time."

"I want you to write to Bill's lawyers about this."

"About what?"

"The fact she was obstructive; that she won't let you go there."

Simon began to get angry. It was bad enough being in bed with 'flu, as he was, without this sort of conversation. "Steady on, Mary."

"Aren't you prepared to help your brother, then?"

The remark had a familiar ring; in an American voice, what's more. Simon groaned. "Are you there?" she asked.

"Yes," he answered wearily.

"Why won't you write to the lawyers?"

"There's nothing to write about; she will see me, but she was not going to be there last weekend."

"It's about time you did something for your brother."

"What was that?"

Mary repeated herself.

"You don't know what you're talking about," Simon said.

"Oh yes, I do."

You're as bad as the last one, Simon thought. "For heaven's sake, Mary! Don't say things like that; you don't know what's gone on in the past."

"What d'you mean? You've never done a darned thing for him; you just want to grab as much of his stuff as you can."

"And commit perjury for him as well," Simon yelled down the telephone. He'd had enough. "I'm not talking to you anymore," he said and hung up. Lying there, with a splitting headache and his limbs aching, he felt exhausted. He couldn't understand why his brother hated him so much, to brainwash Mary like her erstwhile friend, Joan. Whatever led Bill to get involved with women like these? He'd never lacked friends; women found him attractive; Ann said so often. Yet, he preferred to parade himself as the victim, to attract brightly feathered vultures or hopeful vampires at the expense of his family's blood.

A few weeks later Simon drove North to Barmoor. It looked much the same except for a field of grass in front of the house where the lawn used to be. Joan greeted Simon enthusiastically.

"Come in, darling; so good to see you."

Simon recoiled but forced a smile onto his face. Give her credit for something; she'd been very co-operative over his visit.

"Come in and sit down; I want to talk to you."

Now what's happened, he wondered.

"I was talking to my lawyer this morning. Did you know that your dear brother is behind on his maintenance payments? He owes me over £800." She paused to see how Simon would react.

"I'm sorry to hear that," he mumbled.

"Well, never mind. The point is that you can take away £800 of Bill's stuff; it's all perfectly legal."

"Are you sure?"

"Absolutely; I have a lien on his things for that amount; you can give the money to my lawyers if you buy anything."

She got up and fetched a piece of paper. "Here," she said. "Here's the valuation; you look around and find something you like and take it back to London with you."

"What I want more than anything else is the long-case clock in the saloon; hearing it strike reminds me of when I was a boy."

"It's all to be taken away next week, so you'd better be quick. They're sending eight or nine furniture vans from Torquay."

"Why Torquay?"

"I don't know, darling; you'd better ask your brother. He wants everything gone, except he can't have the green drawing-room and my bedroom."

"What'll happen to those things?"

Simon knew the answer before she opened her mouth. "I'll be having it all shipped to New York."

"I'll go and have a walk round then," he said.

Simon left the room and made his way past the landing to the door of the beautiful oval room with the green Chinese wall-paper. He could almost see the shadow of his mother after breakfast writing her letters and books; the delicate marble fireplace with the family coat-of-arms and the mirror above it, the inlaid tables and chairs, the elegant bookcases, tall and dignified even now in their numbered days.

So this was how it would finally end! What wasn't destined to go to New York would end up in an auction room. The house would be stripped of everything down to the last curtain rail. Simon leant against the door; how old and tired he felt; the twenty year fight to save the place was nearly over. Well, he thought, at least Mama isn't alive to witness this. He thought of his sister; just as well she isn't here either to watch the curtain come down. She was so ill, she couldn't take in what was happening; doctors didn't think she had long to live.

He walked slowly round the house; he was almost in tears. To think that what was now happening was due to one man's folly; it could've been avoided. It wasn't even as if Bill had any enjoyment from it, except for one brief period when his Brighton stage friends stayed in the house; and that time when Penelope came to claim his helpful cash. Most people lost their money living beyond their means; Bill too should've blown his money on riotous times in the South of France, giving lavish parties and gorging himself on make-believe. Here there was absolutely nothing to show, except rusting pieces of machinery down at the quarry and a deserted house, ready to fall into decay. With the enormous rooms, empty and cold, in the middle of a Northumbrian winter, unfurnished and unlived in, the Castle was surely doomed.

Picturing the house empty, when the removal men had finished their task, Simon felt a shiver run down his back. The ghosts would take over the hollow echoing shell of the Castle; there'd be the sound of his father's footsteps climbing the stairs to come and say goodnight to him, perhaps even the noise of the old lift at the back of the house as it brought the huge cans of hot water up to the nursery bathroom.

The sound of rain pattering down on the dome above him brought Simon back to his reality. It was pointless to spend so much time dreaming of the past; he still had to drive to London.

He noticed a large decanter with an engraved coat-of-arms.

"What do they say about this, Joan?"

"It's a Waterford, valued at £380; the stopper's missing."

"You're sure it's alright for me to take it?"

"You take it, darling."

"It's a beauty," murmured Simon. He couldn't remember having seen it before, but with so many lovely things everywhere, no wonder he'd never noticed it. "As soon as I get back to London, I'll write to Bill's lawyers and tell them what I've done."

"That's up to you, darling."

They walked down the white stone stairs to the hall. The sticks and riding crops still lay there; the six chairs with their painted crests stood as sentries in the oval outer hall with the old Italian statues spaced between them. He gently placed the decanter inside his overcoat; then put it on the back seat of the car.

"Goodbye, Joan."

"Goodbye, darling.

"I'VE JUST BEEN TALKING to the auctioneers; Barmoor stuff is to be sold at different times." Joan, still in England, was on the phone.

"That's funny," said Simon.

"And they said that not all of it would be sold in London."

"Sounds crazy to me."

"Anyway, darling; I've arranged to send you the catalogues."

"That's very kind of you."

"Come and see me if ever you are in New York."

"Sure." That'll be the day, he said to himself as he hung up.

Two months went by with no sign of the catalogues. Simon discussed their non-appearance with Deborah, his daughter. "Have you had any yet?" he asked her.

"No, but they always take ages."

"I think I'll ring them up, just to be on the safe side."

"Can I come to the sales with you, not that I've any spare cash."

"None of us have," replied Simon.

He got hold of the man at the auctioneers who knew about Barmoor. "I haven't had any catalogues yet; when d'you expect to get them out?" Simon asked

"And it's Mr Sitwell speaking, is it, sir?" said the voice at the other end. "Just a moment, sir."

After a wait of a few minutes the man spoke again. "Are you there, Mr Sitwell? I'm sorry, sir; we are under instructions not to send you any catalogues."

"What d'you mean?"

"We have instructions not to send catalogues to your family."

"And whom, might I ask, gave you these instructions?" asked Simon icily.

"Our principal, sir."

"Your principal?"

"Yes, sir; Mr William Reresby Sitwell of Barmoor Castle."

"I don't believe it! " cried Deborah, when he told her.

"I would," said Simon bitterly.

"Don't worry, Daddy; I'll get them, I'm sure I can. They don't know who I am; they'll think, I'm just plain Mrs Bedford."

"I wouldn't be too sure, but ring them up and ask if the sales have started yet; don't ask about the catalogues straight away."

"Okay, Daddy; be in touch." Simon's daughter was a competent young lady; she'd be able to get to the bottom of things, if anyone could.

Half-an-hour later, the telephone rang. "Daddy!" Simon could almost visualise the exclamation mark hanging in the silence.

"It's not good news, I'm afraid. They've already had two sales."

Simon felt his stomach turn; for a moment he thought he'd be sick. "Go on," he said. "Why haven't you had the catalogues?"

"For the same reason as you; my name was on the list."

"Good God," Simon muttered. This was more than spite; it was obscene! Was Bill revenging his despair, his failure on his family?

"I don't understand it, Daddy. Why is Uncle Bill doing this?"

"His girlfriend the new Mrs Sitwell by now, I'd a row with her."

"But that's no reason for behaving like this."

"You don't know your uncle."

"But what's the point?"

"He's got a rather spiteful nature."

"I think he must be a little bit mad."

"I quite agree."

"What are we going to do, Daddy?"

"I'll talk to my cousin, the real Reresby. He's always helpful and might be able to pull a few strings."

"Have I ever met him?"

"I don't think so, but you should. He's the head of the family and still living at Renishaw."

"I'll try and think of something as well."

Good old Deborah, thought Simon. He knew she'd help him in some way or other; she'd been a pillar of strength over the years.

Not unexpectedly, his cousin Reresby was horrified.

"I'll certainly do what I can; what an appalling story."

"Incredible, isn't it?"

"I haven't seen your brother for years."

"He hasn't been in England a lot; he's mostly in Canada."

Reresby talked for quite some time; the history of his Barmoor cousins had always interested him; he knew that the Sitwells began as the Cytewelles in the 14th Century and that when the family ventured into industry, it was with a large iron-works at Eckington, where they made more nails than any other place in the world and that only discoveries of coal and investments in African mines had saved the family from its later profligacy. Normally Reresby didn't talk about this part of the family history but he was fully cognizant of the chain of events that led to Frank Sitwell inheriting Barmoor. Simon thought it a pity that Reresby had been too young to know Simon's father, the General, as both always wanted to know more about their ancestors.

Reresby was as good as his word; within days he telephoned Simon. "You'll be getting the catalogues," he said.

"Let's have lunch together one day," suggested Simon after he'd thanked him. "There's even more I haven't told you."

A fortnight later, the catalogues started arriving, one every three of four weeks; Deborah was sent them as well.

"They're not much help, actually, are they?" Deborah said.

"It was too much to expect them to mark the Barmoor items, I suppose," said her father.

"You'd have thought they could have put a faint pencil mark, Daddy. You know, anything."

Simon felt tired and fed up; still it was going to be a fight to the finish. "All they say are things like: 'Portrait of an Englishman'. That could be anyone, there are dozens of them."

"Isn't there anyone you know who could go and look for you?"

"Not really, I'll go myself on viewing days to check."

"I'd like the painting of the house that used to hang over the fireplace in the dining-room," said Deborah.

"Let's hope it wasn't in an earlier sales, one we missed."

He heard his daughter sigh. "It is awful, isn't it, Daddy?"

"Yes, I'd like to know why we're supposed to deserve this."

"I hope I never see Uncle Bill again."

"Don't blame you."

Simon went to the sales rooms in London every week. Indeed the catalogue descriptions were so vague as to be virtually useless.

"Why couldn't someone have made a pencil mark against the Barmoor items." Simon asked Isabel, a friend and art dealer.

"They daren't. It's a matter of keeping one's job," she said. "Your cousin did very well getting you catalogues, but I might be able to help a bit too; sometimes I hear things on the grapevine. You'd best tell me what it is that you particularly want."

"Thanks, Isabel. A Walter Russell portrait of my mother; I know that's on the list. And two very nice water-colours of my grandfather and his brother, one of them is carrying a shotgun. There's also a grandfather clock, a set of hall chairs, a wine cooler and a table I'm very fond of."

"Can't you be more specific?"

"Sorry, but I don't know a great deal about furniture."

"Well, I'll do what I can then."

A week later she telephoned. "Furniture items you're looking for are coming up in a sale at Torquay in ten days' time, I think."

"Okay, I'll go down there; thanks awfully."

As luck would have it, Simon also discovered that paintings he wanted were being sold the same day in London. His new wife would have to go and bid for them; only he could recognise the furniture.

Sitting in the fast Inter-City train to the West Country reminded Simon of the days when he had kept a yacht at Salcombe. Stations flashing past opened old pages in his memory.

Newbury: his first wife, Phoebette came from there. Based in Lasham, he'd ridden over to see her on his motorbike. Petrol was too scarce then to run a car for any distance but enough petrol could be scrounged somehow to keep a bike on the road.

How long ago that was, those days of rationing; weekly forays into the countryside in search of eggs, encounters with American aircrews who swopped cigarettes for whisky...

The train stopped briefly at Exeter. He'd been vectored there one night when bad weather made a Lasham landing impossible. It'd seemed like a miracle; the calm voice of the controller taking over, telling him what to do and what course to steer.

"Stay at angels five, course 228; advise your airspeed."

It seemed like yesterday.

"Roger, Jelly two-three; remain on channel B and stand-by."

"Roger, Foxglove."

"Onto channel C, Jelly two-three; call Godown."

"Wilco, out."

"Hullo, Godown."

Half-an-hour later, he was orbiting the Exeter beacon before picking up the Drem lights.

"We're very low on fuel," he told the controller.

"Roger two-three."

"Where the hell are we?" he asked John Hart, his navigator.

"Exeter."

"Hope they give us a decent breakfast," muttered Simon as he selected down on the undercarriage gear.

"They won't be used to operational types like us," replied John.

"There's no point in turning in also; by the time we're debriefed and have breakfast, it'll be daylight," said Simon.

Sitting in the train watching the crowds milling at the doors, he allowed his mind to wander back and recalled the marvellous feeling as he left the aircraft, free at last from the embrace of the parachute harness and the safety straps; pleased to empty his full bladder. Then a long drag on a cigarette. In the movies, admiring WAAF's offering him cups of tea would've surrounded him. Truer to reality, he and the navigator stood shivering by the aircraft and waited for a truck to come round to dispersal and collect them.

"Well, another one crossed off; wonder how the others got on?"

Simon had survived; not so John Hart, father of three. He had crewed up with the C.O. on completing his tour with Simon, as crewing with Squadron-leader Hanbury meant promotion; Simon didn't mind finding a new navigator. John wasn't to know, the move cost him his life; his body soon lay in a wrecked Mosquito somewhere between the Dutch coast and Magdeburg, east of Berlin.

Only that year Simon had been in a train on a Saturday afternoon with a bad headache. He went to the buffet car for a cup of tea to swallow some aspirin. A dozen or so youths were there in near-drunk condition. The old steward cowered behind his counter; empty beer bottles rolled about the floor. It wasn't long before the trouble started. "Who does he think he is, then," one of lads said, pointing at Simon. "Why d'you wear those dark f...ing stupid glasses, Mister?"

Simon stood at the counter with his back to them. He had come through the war more-or-less unscathed except for his eyes; two years of continual night-flying coupled with leaky oxygen masks had made them overly sensitive to light. Outdoors, he always put on tinted glasses.

He stood there pretending not to hear them; the steward took refuge in his little galley. Simon finished his tea and slowly walked out of the carriage looking neither to left nor right, thinking I'm lucky to get away from this lot without a broken bottle shoved in my face. But how ironic! To live through the war; to see his friends die by the score; to face death himself time and time again; just to get beaten up by a bunch of drunken yobboes; the very children he'd gone to war for, unwittingly perhaps, the children he'd helped save from life under the Nazis.

The train pulled out of Exeter. "Next stop Newton Abbot," the announcer said; he'd have to change there for a connection to Torquay. In the sixties, he had changed there for the train to Brent where a little branch line crept through the hills from Kingsbridge to meet the main line.

THE ONE extravagance in Simon's life had been an old steam yacht which he'd kept in the "bag" at Salcombe, up the estuary from Kingsbridge. He'd bought it or the paltry sum of £1000 from a small shipyard in Ayrshire, where it was destined for the breaker's yard. For eight years he'd spent all his spare time restoring it to some resemblance of its former self. During the summer months, he moored it at Salcombe and each winter steamed it up the Channel to Shoreham, where it'd be close to his home in Sussex.

Now, as he looked out of the train at the lovely sweep of the estuary, with the red roofs of Exmouth visible in the distance, and the little yachts lying to their moorings facing the incoming tide, he wondered whether it wasn't the *Norian*, his yacht, which led him to part from Phoebette, his first wife.

An old sailor once told him, it was quite commonplace for men to be in love with their boats; looking back now to twenty years earlier, Simon was inclined to agree. It hadn't seemed so at the time, but he realised now, he'd seriously neglected his wife. In the summer months it wasn't so noticeable; the yacht was chartered most of the time. But, during the winter, he spent all his Sundays at Shoreham working on her. In those days, preservation societies weren't in vogue yet, but a band of paddle-steamer enthusiasts were about. They asked Simon to give a talk on restoring and preserving ancient steamboats. In the early sixties help wasn't available and he was hard-pressed to keep the yacht in good condition.

Now the train ran along the coast, nearly skirting the shoreline. Dawlish, with it's holiday atmosphere, was soon left behind, then Teignmouth and its intriguing little harbour with its narrow entrance from Lyme Bay, that reminded Simon of the Doctor Doo-Little stories; almost a toy of a port with the paragraph ships and the 500 ton continental coasters tied up alongside the busy quay. In a few more minutes the train would be nearing Newton Abbot: it would be time to get out.

"Time to stop dreaming as well," Simon said to himself.

He prepared. The auction was to be held in a rather pretty house on the outskirts of Town. With hours to spare, Simon walked the mile or so, stopping to ask directions. When he arrived, he found the drive lined with Mercedes and Range Rovers mostly, many with foreign number plates.

He'd never been to a country sale before. Seeing so many cars from the Continent already there, and more arriving every minute, filled him with apprehension. It was quite clear already that he was up against professional dealers from abroad with their large bank balances, swelled by the weakness of the pound.

The prospective buyers crowded the rooms, in little groups huddled round some of the nicer pieces, talking together in low voices.

Simon felt as if he hadn't been invited. Many of the well-dressed seemed to know one another; they nodded, smiled, and greeted each other in German and Italian; to them this was just a routine business day. They were there to buy good English antiques, ship them back to the Continent, and resell them from their expensive shops in Europe's capitals. Seeing familiar pieces from Barmoor, uprooted after two hundred years, filled Simon with a mixture of sorrow and anger. He wanted to whisper to those pieces, that they weren't completely alone in this strange house with its view over the English Channel; that they had one friend who would try to rescue them: the dining-room chairs with their old leather seats, the table with leaves that could only be put in and taken out by Thomson. Isolated from its companions was the wine-cooler, that once stood in the window of the dining-room overlooking the pond garden with the ha-ha behind and the fields sloping north to Woodside. He gently stroked the cooler; two foreigners near him peering at it, making notes in the catalogues they carried.

The auction started. It took him an hour to realise that he was completely out of his class, unable to keep up with the bidding on any of the things he wanted. In each case, spending what money he had on the family portraits was more important.

He found an old summerhouse in a corner of the garden, which had a nice view over Torbay; the train for London didn't leave for another three hours. The amalgam of anger, frustration and sadness bore down on him once more. He imagined wealthy dealers in nearby house rubbing their hands over their purchases; the servile removal people and the forwarding agents only too anxious to arrange for the packing and the shipping to smart galleries in Milan or Munich.

"Damn and blast them all," he muttered. He could not help thinking about the war and England's victory; his victory as well. Now, his erstwhile enemies were pillaging his heritage, with the enormous benefit of their strong currencies, unassailably. His thoughts went round and round; first bitterness and anger, soon replaced by a sense of helplessness and unjustness. The Castle had been destroyed from within.

He left the summerhouse and walked to the railway station wondering how he might fill in the time before the train left.

His new wife, Christine, with her fine features and focused energy fit right in at the London art auction and managed to buy two paintings. The one of his mother had come in for fierce bidding, but with her calm confidence, Christine emerged the victor; she'd also bought one of Gordon Ellis' marine paintings. "The water-colours of your grandfather and his brother weren't there," she told him at dinner that evening. "They could've been sold at a sale we didn't know about. I might to be able to attend the next viewing day if you can't manage to," she offered.

"Thanks, but I'll take time off. We'll just have to keep looking."

"If they'd only give us a little help, a hint or something; think of all the time and trouble it'd save us."

"Well, yes, I know, but Isabel's been very helpful; I don't want her to push her luck too far," said Simon. They continued their meal in silence; each thinking about the day's events.

Simon finally managed to buy the water-colours and hall chairs before the money he'd put aside was gone. At another viewing day visit, he found the painting of the house that his daughter wanted. When the day of the auction came, Deborah was there with her husband, as well as Simon with his wife.

"I'll buy it for you; then you can buy it off me later when you've got the money," said Simon.

"If you could do something like that, wonderful. Michael and I can bid up to a thousand but it's bound to go for more."

"Let me do the bidding then; I'll put another seven hundred in to give us a better chance."

"That's super of you, Daddy."

It was no good. Simon went to two thousand pounds, by which time his daughter was tugging at his sleeve and shaking her head.

"Don't worry, Daddy," she said later. "It would've been too big for our house anyway. Tell you what, let's walk down to Fortnums and have some tea." She took his arm. The little group made their way down Bond Street through the afternoon crowds.

Simon and his cousin Reresby at last lunched at Whites over a year after the last auction. "Did you try to get in touch with your brother while this was going on?" asked Reresby.

"I sent three long telex messages to his ship."

"Didn't he reply?"

"He did, he told me to stop telexing him," said Simon bitterly.

"Good Lord! What did you say in them?"

"I can't remember exactly but the gist of it all was that I asked him to sell me a few things privately, and not auction them. I'd have paid him proper prices."

"Well, why wouldn't he?"

"Oh, he's just bloody-minded, Reresby. And lost. He made a slave of himself in the end."

"What an extraordinary business."

"Unbelievable, isn't it?" Simon took a sip of wine. "Yes, you'd imagine that I'd done something terrible to him, wouldn't you? All I've ever done was try to help where I could."

"I don't think I could've helped much either, I hardly knew him," said his cousin. "Come to think of it, I did hear something the other day." He laid down his knife and fork. "I've a friend, a stamp dealer; he's got a little shop behind the Strand, I can easily let you have the address."

"What did he tell you?"

"He was offered several boxes of stuff from a dealer who'd bought them somewhere; he thinks they're Sitwell family things."

"What sort of things?"

"Old letters, Masonic papers, photographs, manuscripts; some of your father's probably; he was quite an important Mason; am I right?"

"Yes, I believe he started a lodge."

"My friend, this chap I'm talking about, said there was a large Bible in one of the boxes."

"A Bible? What would a large Bible be doing there?"

"I agree; I can't believe Bill would have sold the family Bible, those sorts of thing are sacred."

"I'd better go look; I'd recognize it straight away; it belonged to Ann Sitwell. She was Ann Campbell when she married Francis Sitwell in 1795. All of her descendants are written down; it's quite up-to-date, in fact, my name's in it."

"What d'you think happened to it?" asked Reresby.

"I imagine Bill kept it; as you say, it is sacred; like my father's medals. I wrote to Bill long ago about them because I thought Joan had her eye on them, though they'd nothing to do with her."

"What did Bill say?"

"He was very reasonable; said he'd put them in the bank."

"Well, thank goodness for that," sighed Reresby.

They continued with their meal.

"Odd, just how completely different you and your brother are," Reresby said suddenly. "Not that I knew Bill at all, but from what you tell me and judging by what's happened, it's absolutely clear that he has no feeling for the family or anything to do with it."

Simon looked out of the window at the traffic struggling up the slope of St James's Street. He nodded.

"Your brother doesn't appear to have cared tuppence over what happened to anything, and you, on the other hand, are shattered by the whole episode."

"I'm not shattered exactly, but I'll never get over it. Absolute tragedy it is, and the worst of it is, that it needn't have happened."

"What makes you say that?" asked Reresby.

Simon explained about the farm leases. "My mother could have done a lot more too."

"But you told me she sold her paintings and jewellery for him?"

"I didn't mean that; she should've put her foot down to stop him doing the idiotic things he did. And then that business over Anna coming to Barmoor and having a child there; perhaps I'm too old-fashioned, but you can't live in a castle and behave like that," said Simon, warming to his subject.

His cousin smiled. "You're a bit of a prig, you know, Simon."

"No, I'm not; I'm talking about twenty-five years ago. Nobody worries about things like that today; it was different in the fifties."

"I suppose you're right."

"My mother absolutely refused to face facts," Simon went on.

"An annoying characteristic that, I agree," said Reresby.

"Thank goodness, she didn't live to see everything auctioned."

"She was a very great friend of my Aunt Edith's when they were younger, you know."

"I know; she used to stay at Renishaw and Scarborough."

"You've got to remember that her generation saw things quite differently from us, Simon."

"They certainly indulged themselves. Servants did most everything for them. No wonder they'd time to play the piano, speak a couple of languages and sketch endlessly. I've read my mother's diaries. The problems of running a house aren't at all mentioned. Up until the war, she never lifted a finger; when a meal was over, she'd walk out of the room and forget all about it until she was reminded by the gong that it was time to get ready to eat again."

"Speaking of food, what would you like more?"

Simon looked at his watch. "Just some coffee, thank you."

"Very well, let's go into the other rooms."

Reresby led the way from the dining-room at Whites.

"CAN I come with you, Dad?"

Simon sat with his son, Damian, over breakfast, having told him about the visit he proposed making to Reresby's stamp dealer.

"When are we going?" Damian asked.

"After we've eaten. Would you like more?"

"No thanks. Fancy a stamp dealer buying Barmoor things!"

"He probably deals in everything; not just stamps."

Later that morning, they found the shop; on a corner not far from the back of the Savoy hotel.

"I believe you know my cousin, Mr Sitwell," said Simon, by way of introduction.

"That's right, that's right," answered the man, looking Simon up and down. " If you'll pardon my saying so, you don't look alike."

Simon gave a chuckle. "We're very distant cousins; our great-great-grandfathers were brothers."

"What can I do for you, sir?"

"My cousin told me, you'd come across some Sitwell papers."

A puzzled look came over the man's face. Simon thought, don't tell me we've come all this way on a wild goose chase. He glanced at his son who was browsing round the shop. "Don't you have some boxes of papers or something? And I believe there's an old Bible."

"Ah, yes! It's come back to me, I told your cousin I'd happened across them; they're no use to me; if you'll excuse me a moment I'll see if I can find them."

The man disappeared.

"Don't forget to ask him about the medals, Dad," reminded Damian.

The man reappeared carrying a large cardboard box. "Here we are! There are three more like this."

Simon looked through the papers and documents. "How did you come to have this stuff?" he asked.

"I bought it as a job lot, you're never sure what you'll come into; particularly with old families."

"Where's the Bible?"

"One moment, sir; it's downstairs with the other boxes."

"The medals, Dad," reminded Simon.

"All in good time," whispered his father.

"Here we are." The man came back into the room; on top of the box he carried was the Bible. "It's very old," the man said. "Worth quite a bit; but not the sort of stuff I have much call for."

"May I have a look at it?"

"Certainly, sir."

Simon turned back the front cover, then the page next to it. "I'd like to buy it," he said.

"Very well, sir; and what about the boxes of papers?"

"Yes. I'll buy those as well."

"Excuse me then," the man said. " I'll have to look up what I paid for it." He disappeared again. "I could let you have the whole lot for £450," he said, when he returned.

"Very good, I'll write you a cheque now," smiled Simon.

His son caught his eye as he fumbled for his cheque book.

"Here you are." Simon handed him the cheque. "By the way," he added; "were there some medals sold at the same time?"

The man's face lit up. "Oh yes! And what a beautiful set they were," he said enthusiastically.

A feeling of nausea engulfed Simon; he thought he'd have to sit down. "D'you think they were General Sitwell's?" he asked. It seemed a stupid question but there might still be a chance.

Simon glanced at his son who had stopped studying the bookshelves. There was a look of disbelief on his face.

"Yes," answered the man. " You see, I was at the sale but didn't buy anything at the time. The Bible and these boxes were offered to me later; that quite often happens you know."

"Did the auctioneer actually say they were General Sitwell's medals?" asked Simon.

"Yes, I remember quite well; they were such a full set, you see. There were so many campaign medals; quite unique they were. The General, it appeared, served in the Second Afghan War, at Khartoum, in the Transvaal, at Gallipoli, and on the north-west frontier in India, I believe."

"He also commanded the 34th Infantry Brigade at the landing in Suvla Bay during the Great War," Simon said proudly. "Any idea what they were sold for?"

"Let me think now; somewhere in the region of 4000, I believe." Simon shook his head.

"Can we leave this stuff here while we get a taxi?"

"Of course you can, sir."

They left the shop; it was a relief to get into the fresh air again.

"I'll buy the medals, Dad. I've got five thousand saved up if I count your coming-of-age money," said Damian.

"That's very good of you, Damian." He put his arm on his son's shoulder. "But I won't let you. You're going to need every penny you can lay your hands on later on, for your future."

"I'd like to do it, Dad."

"I know how you feel; family medals are special, especially to patriots as you and I have been, but you mustn't."

"Any chance of you being able to buy them?"

"Not at the moment; I'm feeling pretty hard up since those auctions last year; and I've a lot of tax outstanding."

"Let's ask him to try and find out who bought them; then, when you're feeling richer, perhaps you can buy them back."

"No harm in that," replied Simon, but he knew, no amount of money would buy the past back.

They found a taxi and returned to the shop.

"Would it be difficult for you to discover who bought those medals?" Simon asked the man.

"I'll do my best, sir." He stroked his chin. "It's none of my business, sir; but how is it they ever came to be sold? They were your father's, weren't they?"

Simon nodded. They looked at each other; the man shook his head in sympathy with Simon.

"I've only known this sort of thing to happen once before; and I've been in the business a long time."

"We'd better be getting along, the taxi's waiting," said Simon.

"I'll give you a hand with those boxes, sir."

"Thanks; here's my card in case you hear anything."

Father and son sat back in the taxi, the cardboard boxes at their feet; neither spoke.

The driver slid back the window. "Where to, sir?" he asked.

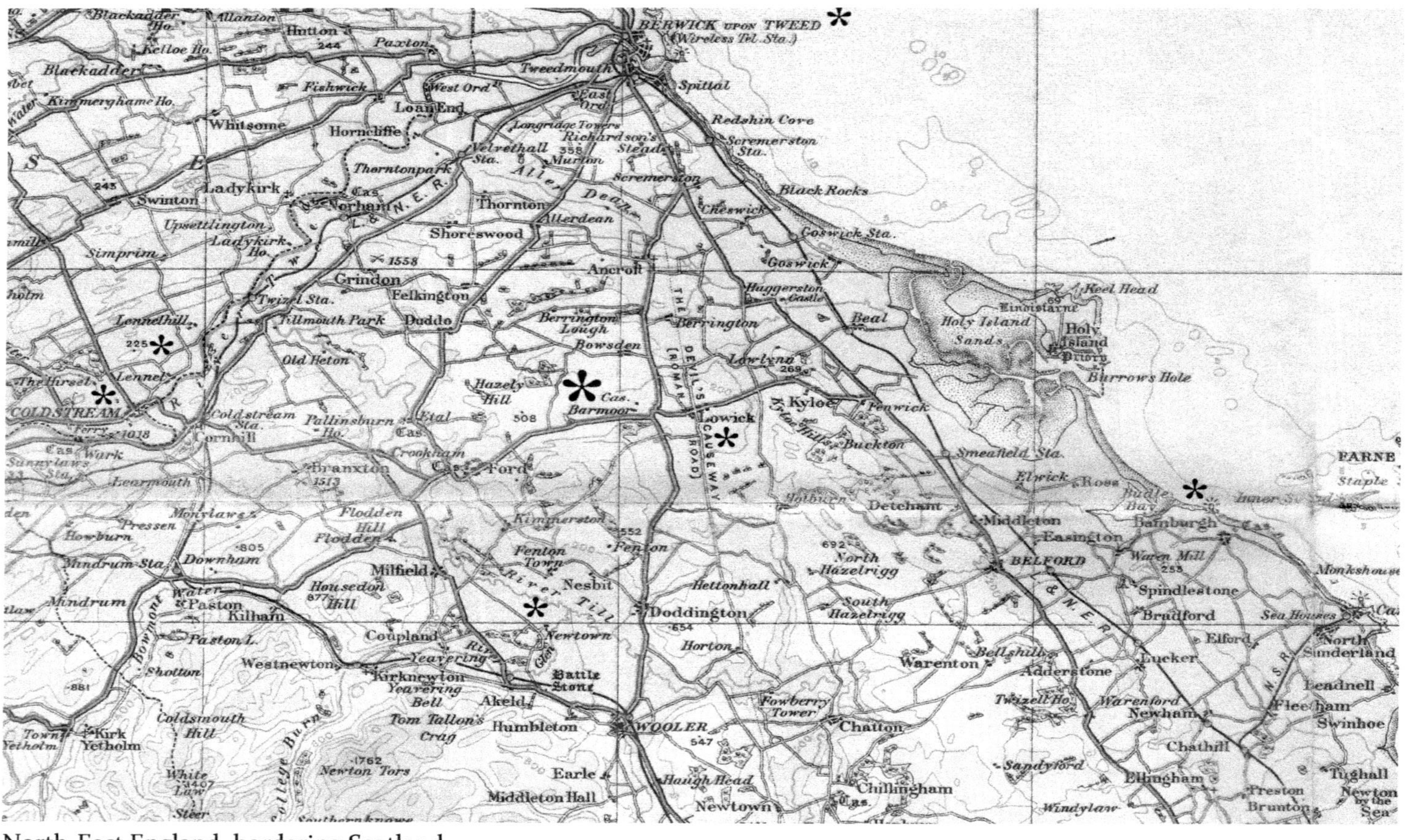

North-East England, bordering Scotland

CPSIA information can be obtained
at www.ICGtesting.com
Printed in the USA
BVHW03*0747190718
521912BV00001B/1/P

9 781939 434654